Workplace Bullying. Does it differ in Faith-Based Organizations?

Written by: Dr. Simone Maxwell-Wilson

DEDICATION

This process has been an indelible journey that wouldn't be possible without the assistance of so many wonderful people. First, I would like to thank God for giving me the strength and courage to write this book. Bina, you may not have realized but you're the person who kept pushing me to consider a PhD. I thank you for being such an encouraging friend. To my mom, where would I be without you figuratively and literally? I recall wanting to take a break and often quit after having Kaylee, but your unwavering support made me unstoppable through those sleepless nights and fatigued days. Mrs. Roberts, I can't thank you enough for all the prayers and the positive words of affirmations; you even sent me flowers to show how much you cared. To my husband, sister, and other immediate family members, I appreciate all the support you've shown me through every step of this process.

Thirdly, to the support staff at Johnson University and my committee members; thank you for believing in me. Dr. Crumpton, you've been like a second mother by offering the tough love when needed yet being supportive and bringing that level of structure to what often seemed like a convoluted process. Dr. Beard, your calm demeanor and logical thinking have helped to take my paper from one that offered nothing new (those words were very impactful ☺) and helped me to dig deeper to find data that can add value to our scholarly world. Dr. Young, your no-nonsense and straightforward approach helped me to develop the confidence I needed to complete my work. Essentially, I could never have done it without you all.

To all participants, thanks for sharing your personal stories about workplace bullying and for being so transparent about a topic that we often try to forget. I hope and pray that my work is a good representation of your stories. I'm thankful for all the intercessory prayers, thoughtful texts, encouraging words and the overall love I received.

FOREWORD

Workplace bullying presents serious challenges to organizations, but it remains one of the most neglected problems in the realm of applied ethics. Accordingly, this book analyzes the lived experiences of six employees who have experienced workplace bullying in Christian organizations specifically in a faith-centered context. First, the investigation described common definitions of workplace bullying, associated behaviors, and the differences between workplace bullying and other negative workplace behaviors. Additionally, the characteristics of workplace bullies and targets, causes and effects of workplace bullying, and the noted preventive measures of workplace bullying were examined in both organizational contexts. Next, six participants were interviewed from varying faith-centered organizations to identify the common themes of workplace bullying in these types of organizations through thematic analysis. Finally, the distinguished threads were assessed to determine the context and specific differences between workplace bullying in general organizations and faith-centered organizations. Future work will need to be completed to determine specific preventive measures of workplace bullying in these types of organizations.

TABLE OF CONTENTS

DEDICATION 2
FOREWORD 4
LIST OF TABLES 7
CHAPTER 1 – INTRODUCTION 8
    Background of the Problem 12
        General Organizational Bullying 12
        Christian Workplace Bullying and Conflict 15
        The Early Church Period 17
        The Patristic Period 17
        The Medieval Period 17
        The Reformation Period 18
    Purpose of the Book 20
    Significance of the Book 20
    Definitions of Key Terms 21
    Overview 23
CHAPTER 2 – BACKGROUND ON WORKPLACE BULLYING 24
    History of Workplace Bullying 24
    Definitions of Workplace Bullying 25
    Types of Workplace Bullying 26
    Workplace Bully Characteristics 32
        Personality 32
        Scientific Findings 34
    Target Characteristics 35
        Personality 35
        Scientific Findings 37
    Causes of Workplace Bullying in Both Organizational Contexts 39
    Organizational Culture and Climate 40
    Balance of Power and Leadership 42
        Autocratic Leadership 42
        Laissez-Faire Leadership 43

Charismatic Leadership	44
Workplace Injustice and Conflict	44
Reward Systems and Competition	46
Group-Based and Cultural Differences	47
Job Insecurity	48
Specific Causes of Bullying in Faith-Centered Organizations	49
Conflict	49
Moral Changes and Spiritualization	50
Effects of Workplace Bullying in the Workplace	52
Job Performance and Emotional Well-Being	53
Health Issues	54
Organizational Costs	54
Specific Effects of Workplace Bullying in Christian Organizations	55
Preventive Measures for Handling Workplace Bullying in Organizations	57
The A-B-C Model	61
Summary	63
CHAPTER 3 – GATHERING THE STORIES	**65**
Research Approach	66
Data Collection Strategies	68
Data Analysis Procedures	73
Validity and Reliability	75
Verification	76
Ethical Considerations	77
Summary	79
CHAPTER 4 – THE LIVED EXPERIENCES	**80**
Findings	80
John's Story	82
Maria's Story	83
Josh's Story	84
Mark's Story	85
Juan's Story	87

    Susan's Story 88
  Thematic Analysis 90
    Theme 1: Bullying Due to Race 90
    Theme 2: Bullying Due to Position and Gender 91
    Theme 3: Bullying Was Spiritualized 92
    Theme 4: Creating an Environment of Failure 93
    Theme 5: Lack of Leadership/Abuse of Power 93
    Theme 6: Fear of Reporting the Bullying 95
    Theme 7: Rebullied as Consequence of Reporting the Experience 96
    Theme 8: Hopelessness and Stress as a Result of the Bullying 96
  Chapter Summary 97
CHAPTER 5 – CONCLUSION 98
  Results in Light of the Study's Research Questions 98
  Comparison of Bullying in Faith-Based and General Organizations 100
  Implications 103
  Conclusion 105
REFERENCES 107

LIST OF TABLES

Table 1. Major Differences Between Workplace Bullying and Harassment 24
Table 2. Managerial Intervention Matrix 57
Table 3. Demographic Information on Research Participants 84

CHAPTER 1 – INTRODUCTION

Bullying is typically a term most commonly associated with academic environments, especially as it pertains to schoolyard bullying. Bullying was identified as a major concern by schools across the United States because at least 15-25% of students reported bullying in various academic environments (Mullin-Rindler, 2003). Schoolyard bullying received more notoriety in all aspects of media, while workplace bullying has not garnered as much attention (Namie & Namie, 2009). One of the main differences between schoolyard bullying and workplace bullying is workplace bullying tends to be less physically harmful but more psychological and verbal in nature (Bartlett & Bartlett, 2011). However, workplace bullying is just as troubling, and leaders need to understand how to mitigate this phenomenon in organizations. Bullying at work is claimed to be a more crippling and devastating problem for employees than all other work-related stress (Einarsen, 1999). Finlan (2015) noted it is often assumed adults are not prone to bullying and can easily resolve their problems, specifically in Christian organizations.

Understanding workplace bullying and the impact on the systemic organizational environment may provide valuable insight to organizational leaders, thereby empowering the organization to engage in positive best practices resulting in more favorable workplace environments (LaVan & Martin, 2008; Lutgen-Sandvik, 2003; Tracy, Lutgen-Sandvik, & Alberts, 2006). Numerous researchers have cited the need for increasing overall societal awareness of the phenomena of workplace bullying and related outcomes (Hodson, Roscigno, & Lopez, 2006; Lutgen-Sandvik, 2003; Namie, 2007; Namie & Namie, 2003). While workplace bullying and harassment are sometimes used interchangeably, the literature has explored the extensive differences between both actions in organizations. Workplace bullying is a behavior described using various concepts and terms, such as mobbing, targetization, emotional abuse, and psychological terror (Lutgen-Sandvik, 2003). On the other hand, Branch, Ramsay and Barker (2013) noted workplace harassment is based on the target's national origin, age, religion, disability, sexual orientation, gender, or other characteristic protected by state and federal laws, and can happen between leaders and subordinates, or subordinate to subordinate. Workplace bullying is most likely to be a top-down phenomenon and affects the relationships between leaders and followers (Namie & Namie, 2009). Bullying at work is claimed to be more crippling and devastating problem for employees than all other work related stress put together (Einarsen, 1999).

Despite the increased studies on workplace bullying, Finlan's (2015) findings indicated very little research was completed on workplace bullying in Christian organizations. The background section will be divided in two sections: workplace bullying in Christian organizations, specifically faith-centered organizations, and workplace bullying in general organizations. First, Christian organizations will be defined as

> organizations that have any of the following: a formal funding or administrative arrangement with a religious authority or authorities; a historical tie of this kind; a specific commitment to act within the dictates of an established Christ-like faith; or a commitment to work together that stems from a common faith and is, not simply based on their personal belief system. (Chaves, 1994, p. 750

Christian organizations can cover a broad array of entities with varying belief systems. Christian organizations are also sometimes described as faith-based agencies (Torry, 2014). Faith-based organizations' main purpose is not religion but can be related in some way to a religious organization or tradition (Sider & Unruh, 2004). The term *faith-based organization* covers an enormously varied field, including tiny community development and youth projects run by volunteers from a congregation with the help of a single paid worker; church schools; denomination-founded housing associations; large nongovernmental organizations (e.g., Christian Aid, Catholic International Development Charity, the Red Cross, and the Red Crescent); Jewish elderly care homes; and the Children's Society and the National Children's Home, founded by the Church of England and the Methodist Church, respectively. Sider and Unruh (2004) suggested there are five types of faith-based organizations:

1. *Faith-permeated* – In these organizations, the connection with religious faith is evident at all levels of mission, staffing, governance, and support. Faith-permeated programs extensively integrate explicitly religious content. The religious dimension is believed to be essential to the program's effectiveness; therefore, participation in religious elements is often required. An example of this would be Catholic Charities (e.g., Cross Catholic Church Outreach and religious congregations).

2. *Faith-centered* – These organizations are founded for a religious purpose, remain strongly connected with the religious community through funding sources and affiliation, and require the governing board and most staff to share the organization's faith commitments. Faith-centered programs incorporate explicitly religious messages and activities but are designed so participants can readily opt out of these activities and still expect the benefits of the program's services. Examples of faith-centered organizations includes Christian universities (e.g., Texas Christian University) and nonprofits (e.g., HOPE International, YMCA, Habitat for Humanity).

3. *Faith-affiliated* – These organizations retain some of the influence of their religious founders (such as in their mission statement) but do not require staff to affirm religious beliefs or practices, except for some board and executive leaders. Although

faith-affiliated programs incorporate little or no explicitly religious content, they may affirm faith in a general way and make spiritual resources available to participants. Faith-affiliated programs may have the intent of conveying a religious message through nonverbal acts of compassion and care. Examples of these include for-profit businesses such as Hobby Lobby and Chick Fil-A.

4. Faith-background – These organizations tend to look and act secular, although they may have a historical tie to a faith tradition. Although religious beliefs may motivate some personnel, faith commitments are not considered in the selection of the staff or board. Faith-background programs have no explicitly religious content aside from their possible location in a religious setting, and they do not expect religious experience to contribute to program outcomes. Examples of this includes Bread for the World.

5. Faith-secular partnership – These organizations present a special case in which a secular (or faith-background) entity joins with one or more congregations or other explicitly religious organizations. This type of organization is typically secular in its administration but relies on the religious partners for volunteer and in-kind support. Leaders and staff respect but do not necessarily share the faith of the religious partners. The programming typically has no explicitly religious content, although volunteers and staff may offer optional religious resources and activities; the faith of the religious partners is considered a program asset whether or not it is expressed explicitly. An example of this includes Friends in Service Here.

For the purpose of this book, research participants in faith-centered organizations that follow biblical or Christian beliefs were examined. Secular or general organizations were not examined (or they were excluded) because they have no reference to religion in their mission or founding history, and they regard it as improper to consider religious commitments as a factor in hiring and governance, plus their programs include no religious content (Sider & Unruh, 2004).

Background of the Problem

General Organizational Bullying

It is presumed workplace bullying has existed since people started working in organizations, but the term is relatively new to U.S. employee relations (Yamada, 2012). Research on the impact of workplace bullying was first conducted during the 1980s by Swedish psychologist, Heinz, who first explored the effects of "mobbing," also known as workplace bullying, among respondents bullied (Leymann, 1990). Leymann (1990) defined mobbing as hostile and unethical behavior toward individuals who were unable to defend themselves. He further described bullying in the workplace as an act of mobbing and likened the term mobbing to when animals in a pack attack a single or larger animal. This phenomenon was identified through Leymann's research; individuals who had experienced bullying in the workplace were at higher risk of becoming depressed, exhibiting signs of anxiety, and displaying symptoms like posttraumatic stress disorder.

A large percentage of research on workplace bullying occurred in European and Nordic countries (Matthiesen & Einarsen, 2007; Rayner & Hoel, 1998) with research in the United States being initially minimal (Lutgen-Sandvik, 2003). British journalist Andrea Adams popularized the term *workplace bullying* in the 1980s and early 1990s using a series of BBC radio documentaries to bring the topic to a more public audience (Matthiesen & Einarsen, 2007). In 1992, A. Adams authored *Bullying at Work: How to Confront and Overcome It,* likely the first book to use "bullying" at work as its operative term (Yamada, 2012). The first study in the United States was conducted by psychiatrist Carroll Brodsky but generated little interest (Einarsen, Hoel, Zapf, & Cooper, 2003).

Ruth and Gary Namie discovered A. Adams (1992), Leymann (1990), and works by other European writers and scholars, and decided campaign of research and education in the United States was necessary to expose this widespread form of common mistreatment at work. Namie and Namie (2003) introduced the term workplace bullying in the U.S. workplace. In response to what Namie and Namie (2009) witnessed and experienced in the workplace, they chose to use the label bullying because they believed it would resonate with the public (Yamada, 2012).

There appears to be agreement in the academic community as to the essential characteristics that define the workplace bullying phenomena, and the academic definitions will align more closely with each other than they will with the professional definitions because more research has been conducted in academia (Branch et al., 2013). These elements were captured in a widely used academic definition, which emanated from Scandinavia and was adapted from Olweus' (1993): "Workplace bullying is a situation in which one or more persons systematically and over a long period of time perceive themselves to be on the receiving end of negative treatment on the part of one or more persons" (p.8).

The definition of workplace bullying is very similar among each researcher with a few slight variations. Workplace bullying was defined by Bartlett (2016) as the malicious verbal mistreatment of a target driven by the bully's desire to control that target. It was further defined as a repeated and enduring act involving an imbalance of power between the target and the perpetrator and included an element of subjectivity on the part of the target in terms of how they view the behavior and its effects (Einarsen et al., 2003). Workplace bullying is also characterized by several features: (a) repetition, (b) duration, (c) escalation, (d) power disparity, and (e) attributed intent (Lutgen-Sandvik, 2003).

There is also a more thorough categorization on what types of behavior constitutes workplace bullying. This helps to clarify the definition so every action or workplace disagreement will not be considered bullying. The major categories of workplace bullying are:

- Verbal bullying: slandering, ridiculing or maligning a person or their family; persistent name calling that is hurtful, insulting, or humiliating; using a person as the butt of jokes; abusive and offensive remarks
- Physical bullying: pushing; shoving; kicking; poking; tripping; assault, or threat of physical assault; damage to a person's work area or property
- Gesture bullying: nonverbal threatening gestures, glances that can convey threatening messages
- Exclusion: socially or physically excluding or disregarding a person in work-related activities
- Cyberbullying: Use of information and communications technology to support deliberate and hostile attempts to hurt, upset, or embarrass another person. Examples include sending abusive e-mails and phone calls, posting comments on websites such as Facebook or Twitter, hacking into other people's accounts, and sending viruses.

    (Carden & Boyd, 2010, p. 145)

In workplace-bullying literature, the bully is referred to as the instigator, and the person being bullied is called the target (Namie & Namie, 2009). A survey conducted by Namie and Namie (2003) stated individuals who were targets of workplace bullying were found to suffer from numerous health issues, including but not limited to anxiety, depression, alcohol and other substance abuse, self-destructive habits, sleep disturbances, and both homicidal and suicidal ideation and tendencies. There is lack of overall knowledge related to complex dynamics involved and the short- and long-term outcomes bullying has on society overall (Lutgen-Sandvik, 2003; Namie, 2007; Namie & Namie, 2003; Simon & Simon, 2006). Witnesses, or those who observe the acts of workplace bullying, can also be adversely impacted.

Additional research is needed to address not only the core definition of workplace bullying but also the underlying preventive causes and factors (Gardner & Johnson, 2001). The research has shown there is no one-size-fits-all approach, but there are certain preventive measures leaders in various organizational sectors can implement to mitigate negative consequences of workplace bullying. For leaders to reduce bullying, it is critical for them to understand how bullying is defined in the context of the workplace and the specific types of bullying that occur in the workplace.

Workplace violence expert Joseph Kinney (1995) noted, "There have been numerous instances where abusive supervisors have baited angry and frustrated employees, pushing these individuals to unacceptable levels of violence and aggression" (p. 132). Although violent or vengeful workers occasionally make the news, there are insidious bullies in nearly every organization, whether coworker, boss, or junior colleague, and their behavior causes other people to suffer shame, humiliation, and fear—all of which can affect their nonwork life and their job performance (Namie & Namie, 2009).

Christian Workplace Bullying and Conflict

Similar to general organizations, workplace bullying also creates challenges in Christian organizations and faith-based agencies. The churches reflect the world, and this world is made up of flawed people; despite the religious rhetoric, human beings are sensitive and will feel hurt when disrespected (Finlan, 2015). Clergy represent a specialized group of U.S. workers providing spiritual, personal, and social services, so the background data and research focus primarily on the church segment of Christian organizations. There are approximately 500,000 Protestant clergy employed in the United States (Association of Religion Data Archives, 2010), with approximately 10% being women (Barna Research Group, 2011). Extrapolating from the Workplace Bullying Institute's (WBI, 2007) estimate of 37% of the U.S. workforce at risk for experiencing some form of abusive workplace behavior, as many as 185,000 clergies could be at risk.

Christian workplace bullying affects organizations that explicitly follow a biblical statement and may become spiritualized when illicit behaviors are rationalized by the superior objective of fulfilling the mission of the institution (Nuñez & Gonzalez, 2009). For instance, since employment in Christian organizations are interwoven with spiritual values, managers or leaders can have the added possibility to use spirituality maliciously as a tool to abuse the targeted individuals who may be reluctant to seek legal advice. As a result, Nuñez and Gonzalez (2009) posited employees may face internal tensions producing psychological effects that are more pronounced than those suffered by employees in other kinds of organizations. This section provides a brief overview of church history that highlights the problem of bullying for the Christian church. It is important to understand how Christian traditions may have contributed to the current day situation of bullying in the Christian organizations. Four historical periods are noted in the discussion: (a) the early church, (b) the patristic period, (c) the medieval period, and (d) the Reformation period. For the focus and purpose of the current research, the four historical periods of the church highlight the problems and some of the historical aspects for each period, regarding Christian history, violence, and forms of bullying (Wetzelberger, 2016).

The Early Church Period

Looking back to original descriptions of bullying in the early church documents, violence and human aggression can be found in the Gospel of Matthew, a passage written between 80 and 90 CE. One passage in Matthew 11:12 (The New King James Version) states, "From the days of John the Baptist until now, the kingdom of heaven has been subjected to violence, and violent people have been raiding it." Matthew's reference to violence and violent people indicates an unfriendly environment in the church from the beginning of time.

The Patristic Period

Following the early church period, the church was subjected to periods of persecution, some of which were state sponsored until Emperor Constantine established religious toleration for Christianity with the Edict of Milan in 313 CE. Saint Augustine of Hippo was perhaps the most prominent theologian in the patristic period, following the reign of Constantine. Augustine played an important role in the development of Western Christianity and philosophy. Vorster (2015) noted Augustine saw evidence in history that the human must be God centered to display true virtue; this is also true about society. Most importantly, this period was characterized by divisions in the Church on matters of theology and doctrine.

The Medieval Period

Eight centuries after Augustine, Saint Thomas Aquinas (1225–1274) was recognized as the leading theologian and natural philosopher of the medieval period. Vorster (2015) wrote:

> Aquinas preached that the love people have for God is the love people should share with one another. He believed "that in creation God bestowed humans with reason and moral capacities that allow humans to advance in moral discoveries and knowledge without special or supernatural grace from God." (as cited in Glanzer & Ream, 2009, p. 34)

Nonetheless, this was a period marked by dissenters in the church because of varying beliefs. Christians, or dissenters, who disagreed with any teachings of their church leaders were either punished or killed (Wetzelberger, 2016).

The Reformation Period

Moving forward another 200 years, Martin Luther was a central theologian of the Reformation. Luther was a professor of biblical exegesis at the University of Wittenberg (Althaus, 1966). During Luther's time at Wittenberg, his separation from the Catholic Church began. Luther experienced firsthand what could be described as a form of bullying, when the Catholic Church excommunicated him for speaking out against his religion. Pope Leo X exiled Luther in 1521 because of his Protestant views, which were condemned as heretical to the positions of the Catholic Church. Violence, in the form of riots, were prevalent in the streets at Wittenberg. It was during this time that Luther was speeding up the reformation. Luther used his passion to create one of the early branches of Protestantism, basing much of his work on the ideas of love and harmony. Augustine and Aquinas affirmed love should be the primary Christian belief, and people should ultimately share love with each other and not treat one another with aggression and hostility. This ongoing emphasis on reducing violence and aggression, through the promotion of love and personal virtue, has continued to be a part of the church's message into the contemporary period.

Bullying is an act that does not demonstrate love for other individuals, and is contrary to the Christian virtue of love, which Jesus commanded when he said, "My command is this: Love each other as I loved you" (John 15:12), or "Love your neighbor as yourself" (Mark 12:31, New International Version). Bullying can happen within the vertical hierarchies of denominations; for instance, districts, regional supervisors, district committees, and pastors can choose to bully someone of lower status to aggressively assert their power (Finlan, 2015). New ideas can be very threatening to religious authorities and bullying can be meant to suppress the target's creativity or theology (Finlan, 2015).

A Christian organization subject to bullying can become weak and unfruitful, and followers will worry challenging bullies is unkind or unchristian (Nuñez & Gonzalez, 2009). Consequently, before followers take any action against bullying or confronting their leaders, the organizational leader typically encourages them to pray for grace, look to Jesus as a healer, and be better, not bitter (Alsgaard, 2013). Some Christian organizations tend to be closed systems, in which people work for administrators they trust but who also hold exclusive organizational power (Wetzelberger, 2016). When there are no mechanisms for objective and independent checks, workplace abuse is more possible and easily rationalized, without employees being able to find help when the system mistreats them (Nuñez & Gonzalez, 2009). Religious people can practice a moralistic and judgmental kind of bullying, commonly recognized as a "holier than thou" attitude (Finlan, 2015). This attitude further results in the common rationalization of bullying in Christian organizations.

Nuñez and Gonzalez (2009) also conducted a study in which employees who worked for Christian faith-centered organizations were interviewed. The interviews indicated both targets and bullies assumed these behaviors are normal and part of the cost the employee must pay to have a job. Overall, the literature agreed on the types of actions considered bullying in both types of organizations but also indicated workplace bullying continues to be a pervasive organizational problem; however, limited studies have been conducted on bullying in Christian faith-based organizations.

Purpose of the Book

The major question was: What are the lived experiences of people who have been bullied in a faith-centered organization? Underlying questions included:

1. What factors contributed to the employee's experiences of being bullied?
2. How did the faith-centered context contribute to the experience?
3. What are the perceived distinctive causes of workplace bullying in faith-centered organizations?
4. What are the effects of workplace bullying in general organizations and faith-centered organizations?
5. Is workplace bullying similar or dissimilar in each of the organizational contexts?

Significance of the Book

Research has shown, while there is no one-size-fits-all approach, there are certain preventive measures leaders in various organizational sectors can implement to mitigate negative consequences of workplace bullying (Bartlett & Bartlett, 2011). Additional research is needed to address not only the core definition of workplace bullying but also the underlying causes and factors to prevent it (Gardner & Johnson, 2001). The fundamental goal of this book was to explore the lived experience of targets of bullying in religious Christian organizations to help understand this demoralizing phenomenon, particularly due to the limited texts in this area.. According to Lutgen-Sandvik (2003), U.S. researchers focused on many negative acts at work, but bullying, as contextualized by the international studies, has not been thoroughly investigated.

Considering the severe consequences of workplace bullying for both the individual and the organization—and potentially even more so for a Christian or general organization—it is important this issue is addressed openly. It is recommended more qualitative research be conducted in Christian organizations and institutions to determine the possible presence and extent of bullying (Nuñez & Gonzalez, 2009). All organizations need to recognize addressing the issue of workplace bullying in a proactive manner, through consistent reinforced policies and effective leadership, is less expensive and practical than to handle the outcomes (Bernardin, 2012).

Definitions of Key Terms

This section will offer definitions of the most commonly used terms related to the phenomenon of workplace bullying to help readers understand key concepts:

Christian organization. Christian organizations are those that have any of the following: (a) a formal funding or administrative arrangement with a religious authority or authorities, (b) a historical tie of this kind, (c) a specific commitment to act within the dictates of an established Christ-like faith, or (d) a commitment to work together that stems from a common faith and is not simply based on their personal belief system (Chaves, 1994).

Downward bullying. Downward bullying occurs when a manager/leader bullies a follower (Branch et al., 2013).

Faith-centered organizations. Faith-centered organizations are founded for a religious purpose, remain strongly connected with the religious community through funding sources and affiliation, and require the governing board and most staff to share the organization's faith commitments. Faith-centered programs incorporate explicitly religious messages and activities but are designed so participants can readily participate (Sider & Unruh, 2004). Examples of this includes Christian universities and religious nonprofit/advocacy organizations.

Follower. A follower is an employee who can be influenced toward the achievement of goals. They embrace change, buy into the vision of the leader, and are inspired to overcome obstacles (Northouse, 2004).

General organizations/workplaces. General organizations/workplaces, for the purpose of this study, are physical locations at which people act together in the course of producing goods and services for an organizational purpose (Masters & Albright, 2002). General organizations have no reference to religion in their mission or founding history, and they regard it as improper to consider religious commitments a factor in hiring and governance. Their programs also include no religious content (Sider & Unruh, 2004).

Horizontal bullying. Horizontal bullying occurs when a follower bullies another follower (Branch et al., 2013).

Instigator. An instigator is an individual who possesses power and identifies another individual to receive systematic, negative workplace treatment that occurs on multiple occasions over an extended period, resulting in psychological and physical consequences for the target (Branch et al., 2013).

Mobbing. Mobbing is the prolonged, malicious harassment of a target, by a group of other members of an organization, to secure removal of the target from the organization (Leymann & Gustafsson, 1996).

Spiritualize. To spiritualize is to give a spiritual meaning to a concept/situation or to understand in a spiritual sense (Nuñez & Gonzalez, 2009).

Target. A target is the recipient of workplace bullying behavior conducted by the bully (Einarsen, 1999).

Workplace bullying. For this study, to be defined as workplace bullying, four criteria must be met: (a) the bullying behavior must occur on multiple occasions over a period, (b) an imbalance of power must be present, (c) the bullying behavior must be focused on one or two individuals, and (d) the bullying behavior must be systematic (Olweus, 1993).

Overview

Phenomenology was a recommended methodology, as the goals were to understand the meanings of human experiences (Creswell, 2013). Bullying is a topic that centers around a lived experience, and phenomenology helped to provide more valuable insights into this social phenomenon in organizational contexts. Phenomenology seeks to expose the implicit structure and meaning of such experiences. It is the search for the "essence of things" that cannot be revealed by ordinary observation (Creswell, 2013).

Additionally, phenomenological research aims to reveal "what it means to be human" (Creswell, 2013, p. 23) and helps researchers develop sensitivity and empathy toward their participants. Bullying is also a very sensitive subject, so this approach was insightful to fairly assess and comprehend the common themes of this concept. Creswell (2013) noted a phenomenological research study can transfer the lived experiences of research participants into sensitive psychological expressions, so the researcher can write about the experiences in a more reflective manner. For my study, I selected eight participants from small- to medium-sized faith-based and faith-permeated Christian organizations, after which I conducted semi structured interviews to collect data on workplace bullying. In the interviews, I used the same tool used in WBI (2007). Upon concluding the interviews, I completed a thematic data analysis to discover pertinent findings on workplace bullying in these types of Christian organizations.

CHAPTER 2 – BACKGROUND ON WORKPLACE BULLYING

Since most texts have focused on bullying in general workplace settings (Brodsky, 1976; Leymann, 1990; Namie & Namie, 2003), this study focused primarily on faith-centered Christian organizations. In this chapter, I discuss literature on types of workplace bullying, causes and effects of workplace bullying in organizational contexts, and a comparative look at bullying in each of the organizational settings. The literature selected for this section includes historical and current information on the topics of interest.

History of Workplace Bullying

The origin of the term workplace bullying can be traced back to Europe (Carden & Boyd, 2010). Mobbing was established as a term in the 1980s by the physician Heinz Leymann (1990). Leymann defined mobbing as hostile and unethical interactions in the work environment, by one or multiple individuals to one individual who is defenseless, after which the term *workplace bullying* was coined by British journalist A. Adams (Namie & Namie, 2009). Additionally, Björkqvist, Österman, and Hjelt-Bäck (1994); Einarsen et al. (2003); Glasø, Matthiesen, Nielsen, and Einarsen (2007); and Hoel and Salin (2003) initiated empirical research in this field, with Scandinavians leading the research endeavor on workplace bullying.

Namie and Namie (2009) brought the term workplace bullying to the United States, in the popular press, in 1998. Bullying at work is a growing field of interest in the academic organizational literature (Liefooghe & Mac Davey, 2010). The number of science-based citations has increased fairly steadily from two in 1993 to 39 by October 2009 (Liefooghe & Mac Davey, 2010). During this time, conferences, special issues (Leymann & Gustafsson, 1996; Liefooghe & Mac Davey, 2010; Sheehan, 1999; Sheehan, Barker, & Rayner, 1999; Zapf & Gross, 2001), and seminar series have brought the issue to international prominence. Interest initially focused on mainland Europe but has spread to North America (Harvey, Heames, Richey, & Leonard, 2006; Keashly, Trott, & Maclean, 1994; Lutgen-Sandvik, 2003). This interest is not confined to academia. Bullying at work is a frequent topic in the popular press, as most organizations have either established or are working to establish antibullying policies (Salin, 2003), and several European countries are either adopting or moving toward some legislation.

Definitions of Workplace Bullying

Per the WBI (2007), workplace bullying is the repeated, health-harming mistreatment of one or more persons (i.e., the targets) by one or more perpetrators that takes one or more of the following forms: (a) verbal abuse; (b) offensive conduct/behaviors, including nonverbal, which are threatening, humiliating, or intimidating; and (c) work interference or sabotage, which prevents work from getting done. Management studies have defined bullying in the workplace as "unwanted, offensive humiliating, undermining behavior towards an individual or groups of employees" (Weisel, 2016, p. 23). Yamada (2000) considered workplace bullying as the "intentional infliction of a hostile work environment upon an employee by a coworker(s) through both verbal and nonverbal behaviors"(para 1).

Einarsen (1999) identified workplace bullying as repeated acts and practices, regardless of being deliberate or not, that affect job performance, create an undesirable work environment, and are offensive and distressing to the victim. On the other hand, Namie and Namie (2003) defined workplace bullying as "the repeated, malicious, health endangering mistreatment of one employee . . . by one or more employees" (p. 23). Lastly, Salin (2003) defined bullying as repeated and persistent negative acts toward one or more individual(s), which involves a perceived power imbalance and creates a hostile work environment (Einarsen et al., 2003; Einarsen & Skogstad, 1996; Zapf, Escartin, Einarsen, Hoel, & Vartian, 2010). Essentially, there are common threads in the definitions of workplace bullying, but a legal definition has not been established to describe this phenomenon.

Types of Workplace Bullying

Labeling of abusive workplace behaviors seems to be somewhat connected to geographical location (Ferris, 2009; Saunders, Huynh, & Goodman-Delahunty, 2007). The term "mobbing" is used in Germanic and Nordic countries (Einarsen et al., 2003; Leymann, 1990), "emotional abuse" is often used in the United States (Keashly et al., 1994; Koonin & Green, 2005), "harassment" is a common descriptor in Finland (Björkqvist et al., 1994), and "workplace bullying" is the term most often used in Australia (Sheehan et al., 1999), the United Kingdom (Rayner & Hoel, 1998), and the United States (Namie & Namie, 2009). While the workplace bullying tactics are similar, the skills adults use to bully each other often involve more manipulation and damaging strategies (Namie & Namie, 2009). The main tactics of workplace bullying, per Oade (2009), have the following classifications: (a) verbal bullying, (b) nonverbal bullying, (c) practical bullying, and (d) performance related bullying. Examples of each are provided here:

- Verbal Bullying Tactics
    - Repeatedly calling a colleague by an insulting name or repeatedly using a nickname they find offensive or dislike to refer to them either behind their back, to their face, or both.
    - Talking about a colleague's performance, character, or conduct behind their back to discredit them in the eyes of their colleagues.
    - Making verbally abusive comments or remarks about a colleague either within earshot or behind their back.

- Repeatedly using verbal aggression, shouting, or swearing when speaking with a colleague.
- Identifying a colleague's mistake, discussing it in public, and overstating their error for the purpose of discrediting them.
- Deliberately choosing to reprimand, put down, or insult a colleague in front of their coworkers.
- Talking about a colleague's performance, character, or conduct behind their back (Oade, 2009).

- Nonverbal Bullying Tactics
  - Using nonverbal signals that denote disapproval or contempt either for a colleague's presence or for their verbal input (e.g., rolling one's eyes, continually staring, laughing at what they say), whether they have made a mistake or not.
  - Repeatedly using nonverbal aggression (e.g., adopting a threatening posture, clenching their fists, glaring at them when speaking with a colleague; Oade, 2009).

- Practical Bullying Tactics
  - Meddling with a colleague's personal possessions or office property (e.g., knocking the potted plant on their desk onto the floor, removing or hiding their folders or files, using their computer without their permission).
  - Using practical jokes to offend or humiliate a colleague in front of their coworkers.
  - Transmitting nasty or insulting text messages, faxes, or e-mails to a colleague, or leaving unpleasant messages on their voicemail system (Oade, 2009).

- Performance-Related Bullying Tactics
    - Continual unwarranted criticism of a colleague's performance or workplace conduct; in some cases, the criticisms are specific, and, in others, they are vague and unclear.
    - Allocating an unreasonable amount of work to a colleague with the intention of setting them up to fail.
    - Purposefully withholding information, a colleague needs to perform effectively in their role—again, to set them up to fail.
    - Suggesting overtly, or through implication, that a colleague's position is under review, that their employment may be terminated, or that they may be demoted for undermining them.
    - Suggesting overtly, or through implication, that a colleague will receive poor appraisal or performance evaluation for undermining them.
    - Selectively applying onerous or petty work rules to one colleague, but not others, to increase the degree of difficulty involved in the first colleague's work, therefore setting them up to fail.
    - Arranging a meeting at a time that is unworkable for a colleague for the purpose of excluding them from the discussion (Oade, 2009).

Despite the different categorizations of bullying behaviors in the literature, the tactics described have vast similarities. Bullying and harassment are sometimes used interchangeably in the literature, so it is important to identify the differences between both terms. Bullying certainly looks and feels like harassment. Harassing, as commonly understood, is defined as systematic, annoying, and continued actions that include threats and demands, and create a hostile situation by uninvited and unwelcome verbal or physical conduct (WBI, 2007). However, at work, harassment is a special term, and workplace harassment connotes sexual misconduct and a hostile work environment (Yamada, 2000). Table 1 lists the major differences between workplace bullying and harassment.

Table 1

Major Differences Between Workplace Bullying and Harassment

Harassment	Workplace Bullying
Has a strong physical component (e.g. contact and touch in all its forms, intrusion into personal space and possessions, damage to possessions including a person's work).	Almost exclusively psychological or organizational but may become physical especially if the bully is male.
Tends to be motivated by an outward personal characteristic of the target, such as gender, race, disability etc.	Tends to be motivated by a hidden personal characteristic of the target, such as competence, popularity or integrity.
A course of conduct constituting harassment can consist of just two incidents.	Bullying tends to be an accumulation of many small incidents, each of which, when taken in isolation and out of context, seems trivial.
The person who is being harassed knows almost straight away they are being harassed.	The person being bullied may not realize it for weeks or months, until there's a moment of enlightenment.
Everyone can recognize harassment.	Few people recognize bullying.
Harassment may involve racist, sexist or other discriminatory vocabulary and actions directed at the target.	Workplace bullying tends to consist of unwarranted criticisms and false allegations, often disguised as management and without openly discriminatory terms. Foul language may be used when there are no witnesses.
Harassment can be for peer approval, bravado, macho image etc.	Tends to be secret behind closed doors with no witnesses.
Acts of harassment at work are obviously not part of work-related communications (e.g., taunting, stalking, vandalizing property).	Acts of bullying are hard to distinguish from work related communications (e.g., making unreasonable demands, making unwarranted criticisms of performance, taking credit for others' work).
The harasser may be content for their target to know they are being harassed.	The bully does not want their target to know they are being bullied.
Harassment is done for the sake of dominating the target.	Bullying is done for the sake of making the bully look more competent than the target.

It is immediately obvious when there has been an act of harassment.	Bullying can be very subtle, so it will not be immediately obvious there has been an act of bullying.

Note. From "Bullying: What Is It? Types of Bullying, Bullying Tactics, How Targets Are Selected, the Difference Between Bullying and Harassment: An Answer to the Question 'Why Me?'," by T. Field and M. Field, 2005. Retrieved from http://www.bullyonline.org/workbully/bully.htm

Table 1 depicts that harassment can be defined as verbal aggression in the workplace that is severe or pervasive enough to create a hostile or abusive work environment based on race, religion, sex, national origin, age, disability, including obesity, military or veteran status, sexual orientation, and other characteristics that describe a person (Field & Field, 2005). State and federal civil rights laws are designed to protect workers from discriminatory, disparate mistreatment, and harassment (Namie & Namie, 2009). Illegal discriminatory harassment occurs in only 20% of bullying cases, which means 80% of bullying is legal unless race, age, or another status group membership characteristic can be claimed (WBI, 2007). Considering this data, workplace bullying is widely pervasive in organizations without any legal ramifications in comparison to harassment.

Harassment is not the only term used synonymously with workplace bullying, mobbing is sometimes used interchangeably and is a form of bullying (Leymann & Gustafsson, 1996). The underlying difference is bullying refers to a single perpetrator targeting an individual for various purposes, and mobbing involves a group of perpetrators targeting an individual for removal from an organization (Sperry, 2009). Davenport, Schwartz, and Elliot (1999) described mobbing as an emotional assault in which a hostile workplace environment is created through innuendo, rumors, and public discrediting. The following are key characteristics of workplace mobbing, per Leymann and Gustafsson (1996):

- Number of perpetrators: This refers to a systematic group process of two or more perpetrators.

- Intentionality: Abusive workplace behavior is purpose driven and goal oriented. Targets are chosen for removal from the organization or workplace setting (Einarsen, 1999; Leymann, 1990).
- Intensity: Mobbing behaviors are a severe form of social stress and more harmful and devastating to targets than other workplace abuses (Hauge, Skogstad, & Einarsen, 2010; Leymann, 1990; Leymann & Gustafsson, 1996; Saunders et al., 2007).
- Duration: Mobbing behaviors are not transient or temporary (Einarsen et al., 2003; Leymann, 1990). Because they are purpose driven and goal oriented, they will persist until the goal of removal is reached (Sperry, 2009).
- Frequency: Mobbing behaviors occur more frequently than other more transient abusive workplace behaviors (Leymann, 1990).

Due to the shared behavioral experiences of being either bullied or mobbed, and the mixed nomenclature in the empirical literature, there were times when the term bullying was used in describing a mobbing dynamic (Cowie, Naylor, Rivers, Smith, & Pereira, 2002; Einarsen, 1999; Ferris, 2009; Zapf & Gross, 2001), and there were times when mobbing described a bullying dynamic (Tengilimoğlu, Akdemir Mansur, & Dziegielewski, 2010). Namie and Namie (2009) described the types of workplace bullies in the following manner:

1. The Screaming Mimi, who is a person who chooses to yell and curse in a public setting. This case is somewhat rare, but it is, in a way, the prototypical bullying scenario.
2. The Constant Critic is concerned with what people do behind closed doors. They are typically bosses who can evaluate and appraise their subordinates. So, when they want to bully a target, they abuse the performance appraisal system. They get a

person behind closed doors and accuse them of bumbling incompetence, when, in fact, that person is more talented, possesses more technical skill, is better liked, and is more ethical and honest than the bully; but, from the bully's perspective, this person poses a threat, and, therefore, they feel they need to attack that person.

3. The Two-Headed Snake involves rumormongering and backstabbing between coworkers. From the boss's point of view, this may mean pitting worker against worker, prohibiting someone from talking to somebody else, or helping somebody on a task, and, sadly, isolating the worker. They will move a bullying target from being colocated to being isolated.

4. The Gatekeeper withholds things people need. For instance, they might deny someone training, even though they have just given them a new job for which they have no skills, and they really need to be taught how to do it. Some other tactics in this category may include denying the target budgetary needs or the pertinent resources for completing their job, such as the correct equipment that sets them up to fail. (pp. 72-73)

For the purpose of this study, unless specifically noted, the terms bully or bullying refer to abusive workplace behaviors by individual(s) common to both an individual bullying experience and a systematic bullying group experience.

Workplace Bully Characteristics

To fully comprehend workplace bullying, it is essential the characteristics of bullies are clearly established. The personality types will be discussed and the leadership styles associated with workplace bullying behavior.

Personality

While violent or vengeful workers occasionally make the news, there are insidious bullies in nearly every organization, whether a coworker, boss, or junior colleague; their behavior causes other people to suffer shame, humiliation, and fear, all of which can affect their nonwork life and their job performance (Namie & Namie, 2009). In the United States, workplace bullying appears to be a very top-down phenomenon and disproportionately harmful to female workers (WBI, 2007). The WBI/Zogby survey found "72 percent of bullies are bosses, and 55 percent of those bullied are rank-and-file workers" (Yamada, 2000, para. 3). Rayner and Hoel (1998) indicated men and women reported victimization at the same rate; however, the WBI (2007) reported 69% of bullies are men, while 31% of bullies are female. When the bully is female, she chooses a female target 68% of the time. Male bullies choose female targets 57% of the time and male targets 43% of the time (WBI, 2007). The gender preferences speak to the power imbalance characteristic of workplace bullying (Namie, 2007). Given the statistics of male victims, female victims historically report bullying at a higher rate than male victims (WBI, 2007).

Based on the review of Samnani and Singh (2016), five characteristics were identified that tend to predict the enactment of aggressive behavior: (a) trait anger, (b) narcissism, (c) envy, (d) aggressiveness, and (e) perceptions of injustice. These characteristics will stimulate perpetrator's moral emotions, which will then lead them to engage in bullying behaviors (Samnani & Singh, 2016). A 2010 survey conducted by the WBI stated 37% of the U.S. workforce, or 53.5 million people, have directly experienced bullying or repeated mistreatments by one or more employees that takes the form of verbal abuse, threats, intimidation, humiliation, or sabotage of work experience, and an additional 15% said they have witnessed bullying at work (WB1, 2007). While there are mean and abrasive characters in the workplace preying on others' vulnerabilities, often bullying can be unintentional. Namie and Namie (2009) asserted this behavior can stem from a lack of self-awareness and poor emotional intelligence, or it can be the result of overused strengths of passion, aggressive style, or forceful expression. Peers, managers, and bosses can cross over into bullying, particularly when problems surface (Namie & Namie, 2009); therefore, these personal attributes can be contributing factors to intentional/unintentional workplace bullying behaviors but are not the key determining factors.

Scientific Findings

The research on childhood bullying places the percentage of children who have bullying personal characteristics at 7-15% of the school age population (Harvey et al., 2006). The rationale for the nature argument (i.e., born with aggressive and/or antisocial characteristics), relative to the causes of becoming a bully, center on gene defects and the absorption of essential hormones in the brain (Harvey et al., 2006). It was assumed there is a biological connection between inherited characteristics and aggression, as several studies were completed in Denmark, Holland, Sweden, Great Britain, Australia, Japan, Canada, and the United States.

From these countrywide studies, there would appear to be three leading biological causes of aggression and the potential for being a bully as an adult. First, brain-related issues, where the frontal lobes of the brain are thought to influence self-control, maturity, judgment, tactfulness, reasoning, and aggression and the prefrontal cortex uptake of glucose (i.e., the fuel for the brain) is significantly lower for antisocial aggressive individuals (Raine et al., 1994). Second is the mutation of specific genes; researchers have discovered in impulsive aggressive males a mutation in genes that codes for an enzyme, monoamine oxidase A. This gene metabolizes serotonin, dopamine, and norepinephrine in the brain. If the gene malfunctions and does not metabolize the appropriate amount of these chemicals, high levels of aggression and antisocial (e.g., bullying) behavior can occur (Harvey et al., 2006). It is also thought genotypes can moderate children's sensitivity to environmental stress and insults that might lead to antisocial bullying on their part in group settings (Caspi et al., 2002). Third is an overly developed immune system. Researchers found aggressive behavior is associated with a strong immune system with aggression-immunity association strongest for CD4 cells and B lymphocytes (Booth, Johnson, Granger, Crouter, & McHale, 2003). Essentially, increasing evidence suggests the immune system is involved in responses to social stress in adulthood.

A final argument and rationale for individuals becoming adult bullies in the workplace is that they were bullied as children (Bosworth, Espelage, & Simon, 1999). Bullying may be an imitation of experiences these individuals had at home (i.e., from parents, siblings, or caregivers) or in their educational/social life (Haynie et al., 2001). The literature on child abuse indicates abused children have a higher propensity to be abusers when they become adults (Bosworth et al., 1999). It is important to note bullies are rarely psychopathic (Murray & Segal, 1994). Harvey et al. (2006) noted a majority of those who bully are opportunistic and have an acute ability to read situational cues and act upon them. Bullies may be ignorant to normative social skills, but they certainly are not stupid. The political skills possessed by the bully are generally well developed and allow them to enact the bullying event while at the same time avoid sanctions or negative reactions coming from others in the organization.

Target Characteristics

Every workplace target is different, but they share commonalities described in the following sections. Since targets were the basis of this study, understanding their characteristics is of vital importance. Specific personality traits and scientific findings of targets are discussed.

Personality

First, "nice people" are often targeted because bullies figure nice people are unlikely "to confront or stop them" (Yamada, 2000, para. 2). Namie and Namie (2009) noted targets are often blessed or cursed with a strong work ethic and just want to be left alone to do their work. The most bullying-prone industries tend to be those fields (e.g., healthcare, education, and public service industries) where stressful conditions and rigid hierarchical structures create environments and where many employees share a prosocial orientation and are the "do gooders" (Namie, 2007). They want to heal the sick, teach and develop the young, care for the elderly, and work with the addicted and abused in society. Because of their tender hearts, they may be ripe for exploitation. While they focus on doing good and noble things awaiting reward for their quality work, they expose themselves to the bully. A follower becomes a target when the bully tests their humiliating tactics on several people at work and the target does not fight back or confront the bully immediately (Namie & Namie, 2009). These surprising findings suggest employees may punish overperforming coworkers in an effort to force them into lowering the bar (Einarsen, 1999).

Glasø et al. (2007) focused on whether there was a typical personality profile for bullied employees. Coyne, Craig, and Smith-Lee Chong (2004) approached workplace bullying from a team context, examining firefighter teams. Surveys were given to personnel to self-identify both bullies' and targets' self-identification. Questions were asked about formal and informal networks in the organization. Results indicated most targets were often isolated in teams, thus resulting in workplace bullying affecting team effectiveness. Targets may be independent, more technically skilled than their bullies, better liked, have more social skills, and quite likely possess greater emotional intelligence and empathy, even for their bullies, but they refuse to be subservient (Namie & Namie, 2009). Some may be "go-to," ethical, and honest veteran workers to whom new employees turn for guidance. Some may be targets who are guileless or are whistleblowers who expose fraudulent practices (Namie & Namie, 2009).

There is one group of bullying targets that does not fit the stereotypical profile of the weak and unconnected individual. In some rare cases, the target of the bully is a true rival of the bully in the workplace setting. It can be another strong individual who competes with the bully for control of the formal or informal organization (Namie & Namie, 2009). What is frequently referred to as an "elephant fight" or the" battle of the giants" occurs when two strong rivals fight for control over the work environment, very much like the establishment of an alpha male in a pack of wolves (Brodsky, 1976). Managers who attempt to change organizational culture fit this classification. The target is the loser of the battle, and, if they stay in the organization, they may be continually bullied because the alpha is driven to maintain control. This can be seen in the top management of organizations, when rivals strive to be named chief executive officer or chairman of the board (Morrill, 1992). The loser frequently is publicly humiliated and run out of the organization. It is also noted some targets may be bullied due to high self-esteem, and they were described as overachievers with an unrealistic view both of their own abilities, resources, and the demands of their work tasks (Brodsky, 1976). By viewing themselves as more accurate, honest, and punctual than their colleagues (Zapf & Gross, 2001), this behavior allows the target to be perceived as too perfect, which leads to bullying.

Scientific Findings

Harvey et al. (2006) provided research findings related to those who are targets of workplace bullying:

1. A convenient starting point in evaluating the common denominators of bullied individuals is grouping them into low self-esteem individuals versus high-self-

esteem individuals (Schwartz, Dodge, & Coie, 2003). That self-esteem is a composition of five dimensions (i.e., cognitive ability, emotional stability and maturity, professional and personal accomplishments, the character of the target and support from peers, and physical characteristics of the target). The potential bullying target may have high marks on only two or three of the self-esteem dimensions; however, with an uncanny sixth sense, the bully will zero in on the dimensions in which the potential target is vulnerable. Thus, they can successfully attack the individual and keep the low self-esteem panic button pushed (Aquino, 2000; Aquino & Byron, 2002).

2. Targets or bullied individuals may appear to be passive and not well connected in the organization. They are frequently considered to be in the "out group" (e.g., those individuals who have little power or respect in the organization because they are not accepted by key individuals; Aquino & Byron, 2002). This lack of status in the organization can become a self-perpetuating cycle, and, if supported by others in the organization, the bullied individuals can experience learned helplessness (e.g., the target expects to be bullied because of their lack of status and low self-esteem they think it is only natural; Miller & Seligman, 1975). Unfortunately, change agents and new hires may fit this category.

3. Vulnerable individuals may have a history of being targets of bullies on the playground and in business organizations (Coyne, Seigne, & Randall, 2000). Many bullied individuals have a predisposition to negativity, which lends itself to becoming or remaining a target to be bullied (Felson & Steadman, 1983; Olweus, 1993; Schwartz et al., 2003).

4. There are conflicting results for age, with some researchers finding older employees are more likely to be bullied than younger employees (Einarsen & Skogstad, 1996). A study by the WBI (2007) found the average age for workplace bullying targets is 41. One of the reasons for ageist workplace bullying is some employers may want to drive out more experienced workers who typically are paid more (Namie & Namie, 2009).

5. Tepper, Moss, and Duffy (2011) found, when supervisors perceive subordinates are different from themselves, those differences lead to higher levels of relationship conflict, which, in turn, is associated with higher levels of bullying from the leader toward the followers; however, this mediated relationship was stronger when supervisors perceived subordinates to be lower performers. That is, lower performing subordinates seem to be at higher risk of mistreatment from supervisors.

Causes of Workplace Bullying in Both Organizational Contexts

There is no definitive map in any organization that will identify where workplace bullying occurs, but there are certain scenarios and contextual factors that increase the proclivity of one to bully another. Hutchinson, Wilkes, Jackson, and Vickers (2010) found bullying is more prevalent in organizations where there are (a) informal organizational alliances; (b) organizational tolerance and reward; and (c) misuse of legitimate authority, processes, and procedures. In addition to these findings, the research has indicated organizational culture and climate, balance of power and leadership, workplace injustice and conflict, reward systems and competition, group-based and cultural differences, and job insecurity are the major influences of bullying in the workplace (Hutchinson et al., 2010).

Organizational Culture and Climate

Baron and Nueman (1998) found popular cost-cutting measures such as downsizing, layoffs, and organizational changes (e.g., corporate restructuring) were significantly related to acts of "verbal aggression and obstructionism" (Baron & Nueman, 1998, p. 395) in the workplace. Hornstein (1996), examining the corporate work environment of the early 1990s, described a siege mentality whereby managers felt "they must stamp down subordinates to stay on top of things and alive" (p. 29). This environment "ignited explosions of brutality both from innate bullies who thrive on their mistreatment of others and from overburdened bosses who might never have behaved that way in less stressful times" (Hornstein, 1996, p. 143). Hence, corporate interpersonal relationships are also considered one of the key factors of workplace bullying based on the research data. While these interpersonal communicative processes are clearly important, the focus of significant research group characteristics have only recently begun to be expanded (Ramsay, Troth, & Branch, 2011). There appears to be a confluence of dynamics taking place over the last couple of decades that accelerated the rate and severity of bullying activities in the workplace (Sheehan et al., 1999). First, the pressure of unprecedented change in business (e.g., globalization, hypercompetition, consolidation, outsourcing, increased regulation of business, and an increase in the rate of technological change) created a level of uncertainty, which was described by some authors as "competing on the edge of chaos" (Hamel & Prahalad, 1994, p. 27; Hitt, Keats, & DeMarie, 1998, p. 31). Second, significant time pressures on managers to accomplish tasks that traditionally took months to complete now must be completed in just weeks (Harvey et al., 2006).

The relationship between the role of the organization and the existence of bullying was stated clearly since the initial studies by Leymann (1990). Also, Hoel, Glasø, Hetland, Cooper, and Einarsen (2010) indicated relationship-oriented factors (e.g., interpersonal conflict, leadership behavior, role conflict, and organizational climate) are very strong independent predictors of bullying at the workplace, while task-oriented factors, in the form of decision authority and job demands, show weaker but significant relationships with workplace bullying. Fox and Stallworth (2005) showed a stressful work environment may result in aggressive behavior due to the individual's negative effect, thus encouraging perpetrators to be engaged in bullying behavior. Also, Baillien, Neyens, De Witte, and De Cuyper (2009) found, in informal work atmospheres where humiliating jokes, surprises, and insults are a part of the socialization, bullying is likely to happen to targets who do not seem to be happy or part of the shared norms.

Bullying that happens due to organizational leaders' unwillingness, or inability to address this phenomenon, effectively can lead to incivility spirals contributing to a toxic organizational climate (Andersson & Pearson, 1999). The organizational climate plays a significant role in whether workplace bullying is occurring in the organization. Bartlett and Bartlett (2011) and Harvey et al. (2006) found bullying is much more likely to happen if the bully feels the organizational climate grants them the blessing to bully. Furthermore, workplace bullying was reported to negatively affect the target's relationship with peers and supervisors (Glasø et al., 2007), lower teamwork (Baillien et al., 2009; Gardner & Johnson, 2001), reduce morale (Namie & Namie, 2003), and decrease organizational commitment (Gardner & Johnson, 2001), all of which have significant implications for an organization's culture. Yamada (2012) addressed how workplace bullying impacts organizational leadership and presented measures leaders can use to tackle this problem.

Balance of Power and Leadership

Organizations characterized by a strict focus on power relations, formal atmosphere, and extreme goal orientation can be associated with workplace bullying (Einarsen et al., 2003); however, leadership style emerged as another important situational factor in the workplace bullying phenomenon. For example, targets of workplace bullying tend to report having leaders who are less charismatic (Hepworth & Towler, 2004) and more abusive (Mitchell & Ambrose, 2007), and targets tend to report having leaders who are less fair and supportive (Hauge et al., 2010). In a study of more than 5,000 British employees, Hoel et al. (2010) found bullying was positively associated with noncontigent punishment, a leadership style where punishment is used arbitrarily; therefore, punishment that is administered arbitrarily can contribute to bullying. Autocratic leadership, laissez-faire leadership, and any other authoritarian leadership style appears to be fertile ground of workplace bullying (Einarsen, 1999). Contrarily, bullying has been negatively associated with a participative leadership style. Victims bullied by their superiors also seem to suffer more in psychological terms than victims of peer-to-peer bullying (Hoel & Salin, 2003) due to an imbalance of power.

Namie (2007) highlighted that leaders lacking the interpersonal skills of listening, coaching, effective training, and caring for workers tend to supervise aggressively to mask their incompetence, which can result in workplace bullying. Autocratic, laissez-faire, and charismatic leadership styles will be further examined to determine why their attributes are more likely to be associated with workplace bullying.

Autocratic Leadership

Although the findings indicate managers and leaders are of central importance in the bullying process, very little research has examined how managers react when bullying develops in their work group (Hoel & Salin, 2003). This is partly because some of the current approaches to understanding the development of bullying examine the manager's role over a relatively long-term period (Hoel & Salin, 2003). An autocratic manager who exerts their authority inappropriately may be bullying their staff, even if this is not intentional. Often the controlling manager does not realize some their behaviors may be bullying, may justify them as reasonable management practice, and may believe their staff is too sensitive (Jenkins, 2013). It is typical to see autocratic leadership as being at one end of a continuum, focusing on compliance and delegation at the other (Yukl, 2000). Autocratic leadership is often used synonymously with a directive or even a coercive style of leadership, although its potency in terms of how it is operationalized varies from relatively moderate to relatively extreme levels (Yukl, 2000).

Laissez-Faire Leadership

Some laissez-faire managers are intimidated by members of their team and tend to not get involved when there is conflict or inappropriate behaviors (Yukl, 2000). They often delegate all of their managerial responsibilities to others (Jenkins, 2013). Managers who are very slack or have a laissez-faire attitude can also contribute to workplace bullying because they fail to properly supervise or guide workers, provide adequate feedback, or address poor performance or behavior problems (Jenkins, 2013). Microlevel day-to-day interactions between bullying targets and their leaders have received limited attention. Poor management skills or low levels of support are expected over time to enable staff to bully, and destructive or laissez-faire leadership styles are viewed as relatively stable patterns of behavior that can lead, over time, to the perception of either bullying by the manager or to a situation where rules are no longer respected in the workplace and bullying is tolerated (Woodrow & Guest, 2017). Overall, research findings have indicated laissez-fare leadership is positively related to bullying in the workplace (Nielsen & Einarsen, 2012).

Charismatic Leadership

Charismatic leadership is also sometimes associated with workplace bullying (Namie & Namie, 2009), and charisma can have its disadvantages. R. Hogan, Raskin, and Fazzini (1990) discovered some top executives who look good to their peers and their bosses, and who do well on most assessments, can sometimes not be good for company's overall leadership. R. Hogan et al. (1990) also claimed these are flawed managers whose glittering image masks a dark, destructive side. These charismatic managers end up being costly by creating poor morale, excessive turnover, and reductions in productivity, potentially ruining a company through their behavior. Some charismatic leaders bully because they are afraid of seeing their own shortcomings exposed, and they often feel threatened by the abilities or career ambitions of the people they bully, opting to use them as scapegoats (Bartlett, 2016). Bartlett (2016) further noted the target may also delay action, hoping, with the passage of time, the bully will stop, and, unfortunately, the bully may interpret all inaction as submission.

Workplace Injustice and Conflict

Role conflict, role ambiguity, and lack of clear goals are features of work organizations that, as early as the 1990s, were found to be linked to bullying (Einarsen, 1999; Vartia, 2001); therefore, bullying thrives where employees perceive contradictory expectations, demands, and values in their jobs, and where expectations are perceived as unclear or unpredictable (Einarsen et al., 2003). This finding is confirmed by a meta-analysis of empirical studies between 1987 and 2005, which included 90 separate samples and concluded role conflict and role ambiguity were among the strongest predictors of workplace bullying (Bowling & Beehr, 2006). Traditional employment relationships have now given way to more part-time work in today's modern workforce, and, as such, loyalty to one employer becomes difficult. There is also no chance to develop the interpersonal bonds that form when people stay together over time, and the result is a leaner, meaner workplace atmosphere in which bullying is more apt to happen (Yamada, 2012).

Bullying also presents itself when a high degree of pressure is present in a work environment that offers employees little control over their own work. This equates to Karasek's (1979) job demand-control model of stress in which strain is seen as the likely outcome of a combination of high demand and low decision latitude (Einarsen et al., 2003). Also, physical aspects of the work environment such as noisy, hot or cold circumstances, or cramped conditions were found to be an antecedent of bullying (Einarsen, 1999). Similarly, a qualitative study by Baillien et al. (2009) found working in high temperatures, crowded spaces, or otherwise unpleasant and irritating environments, and relying on sharing tools and equipment, were all associated with higher risk for bullying.

Finally, meta-analytic evidence showed workplace injustice is another key predictor of aggressive behavior at work (Hershcovis, Reich, Parker, & Bozeman, 2012). The organizational justice literature focuses on three main types of justice: (a) interpersonal, (b) procedural, and (c) distributive. Interpersonal justice refers to the quality of the interpersonal treatment people receive when supervisors make decisions and implement procedures (Bies & Moag, 1986). Procedural justice refers to the fairness of the procedures used to determine organizational outcomes (Leventhal, 1980). Distributive justice refers to the fairness of the actual outcomes and decisions made by supervisors (J. S. Adams, 1965). Hershcovis et al. (2012) found all three forms of injustice were related to employee aggression and workplace bullying. Despite this, interpersonal injustice had the strongest relationship with employee aggressive behavior, followed by procedural and then distributive justice. Perhaps contrary to popular belief, employees appear to be more concerned with the respect and dignity with which supervisors communicate outcomes and decisions than they are about the fairness of the outcome itself (Hershcovis et al., 2012).

Reward Systems and Competition

The factors discussed so far are considered possible enabling factors, which are factors that create the opportunity for bullying to occur in the first place (Einarsen et al., 2003). Salin (2003) also provided the roles of motivating factors that create an incentive for a bully to engage in such behavior. For example, in sectors and countries characterized by strict employment laws, bullying may be a way to expel undesired employees (International Herald Tribune, 2004). This is often seen in the public sector when bullying is used as a strategy for circumventing rules and eliminating unwanted persons (Salin, 2003; Zapf et al., 2010).

Regarding how different reward systems cause workplace bullying, Salin (2003) found bullying may sometimes be used as a micropolitical strategy to enhance the bully's own position in the organization. In very competitive work environments, bullying may be used strategically to punish or get rid of over or underachieving followers or colleagues who are considered burdens or threats (Salin, 2003). In a Finnish study, Sutela and Lehto (1998) reported performance-based rewards systems increased the risk for workplace bullying. For instance, bullying may be used not only to sabotage the work performance of others but also to achieve compliance to meet organizational goals and objectives. Accordingly, Collinson (1988) noted the introduction of collective bonus systems may reinforce some leaders concerns about controlling their employees, thus resulting in bullying. Bullying caused by motivational factors, rewards systems, and competition may result in higher pay, increased promotional opportunities, and improved performance appraisals for the bully (Salin, 2003). The target in turn fails to attain these accomplishments and incentives in the organization.

Group-Based and Cultural Differences

The literature indicates group-based differences sometimes appear to be the only reason people are bullied (e.g., minority groups who have race and ethnicity as "visible markers" are likely to be more vulnerable; Cortina, 2008; Fox & Stallworth, 2005; Lewis & Gunn, 2007; Roscigno, Lopez, & Hodson, 2009). More broadly, Roscigno et al. (2009) found groups occupying structural positions (e.g., entry-level roles) associated with little power, which are also more likely to be linked with minority groups, were at greater risk of being bullied. Researchers have also found mixed results for ethnicity. To illustrate, while Lewis and Gunn (2007) found ethnic minorities are more likely to experience bullying than White employees. Fox and Stallworth (2005) found no significant differences between White, Black, and Asian employees. Baron and Nueman (1998) explained people tend to be

> attracted to others they perceive as being similar to themselves and repulsed by those who they view as being dissimilar. When people with diverse characteristics are compelled to work together, 'decreased levels of interpersonal attraction and increased potential for aggression' may be the result, especially if diversity is not properly managed, thus resulting in bullying. (p. 15)

Another perspective in the workplace bullying literature is the possibility of broad differences based on national culture (Escartín, Zapf, Arrieta, & Rodriguez-Carballeira, 2011). One reason this phenomenon is more prevalent in the U.S. workforce is the individualistic culture in the United States (Tracy et al., 2006). While the cross-cultural perspective presents a complex area that is difficult to research, one recent study investigated perceptual differences of workplace bullying in the two world regions of Central America (i.e., Costa Rica) and Southern Europe (i.e., Spain; Escartín et al., 2011). Though there were many similarities in the understanding of workplace bullying, employees from Central America placed more emphasis on the physical component of bullying compared to their European counterparts. Further research is needed on this level of understanding of workplace bullying (Branch et al., 2013). Workplace diversity steadily increased, and this can also accentuate the differences among employees in an organization. The introduction of women, minorities, foreign employees, and more educated employees potentially heightens the tension felt between these different groups, and, in response to changes in diversity, one group may attempt to exert their power over other groups in the organization (Crawford, 1999).

Job Insecurity

Baillien et al.'s (2009) research examined the relationship between the job stressor, job insecurity, and workplace bullying. Their research indicated there is a correlation between job insecurity and bullying and being a target of a bully. In both instances, because the employee is unsure of their job status, they may lash out at other employees or become a target of a bully due to fear of job loss (Baillien et al., 2009). There are several reasons that hint at a relationship between job insecurity and workplace bullying in general and between job insecurity and targets' and perpetrators' reports of workplace bullying (Yamada, 2000). Job insecurity resides in a climate of gossip or rumor (Bordia, Hobman, Jones, Gallois, & Callan, 2004) and a climate thought to permit or even to stimulate workplace bullying (Baillien et al., 2009). Furthermore, job insecurity creates a climate of rivalry when employees see colleagues as potential rivals for jobs. The argument that supports the relationship between job insecurity and being a target of workplace bullying is that job insecurity likely wears out the employees' resources, which could imply employees offer little resistance against unfair treatment and workplace bullying (Hoel & Salin, 2003); hence, they are easy targets.

Per Yamada (2012), the global marketplace places increasing pressure on managers and workers to provide more and better goods and services at a lower cost. These stressful elements fuel natural bullies and create new ones. Companies' tendency to adopt a downsizing mentality has exacerbated the problem, for those retained are often expected to produce more with fewer resources. Some managers have developed a siege mentality and believe they must clamp down on subordinates to stay on top of things; bullying can be a natural result of this (Yamada, 2012).

Specific Causes of Bullying in Faith-Centered Organizations

Bullying in faith-centered organizations can happen as a result of the same factors in general organizations. While one might think churches and faith-based entities organized with the purpose of disseminating ethical values and principles based on the Bible would be exempt from mistreating employees, no human enterprise is free of workplace bullying, not even organizations that by definition and vocation should manifest more ethical behaviors (Nuñez & Gonzalez, 2009). Because of the values Christians are supposed to hold, bullying in Christian denominations and organizations tends to come as a shock to employees and has the potential to create even greater devastation for the targeted individual (Nuñez & Gonzalez, 2009). Nonetheless, there are specific causes of workplace bullying in faith-centered types of organizations, including conflict and moral changes.

Conflict

Conflicts in Christian organizations sometimes result over matters of principles, the way the world works, different callings, assets, control, mission work, political advocacy, what is true and false about God, and loyalties (Alsgaard, 2013). When conflict takes places, Christian organizations normally disseminate ethical values and principles based on the Bible, which may exempt human resources' protocol on handling peer-to-peer or management-to-peer conflict (Nuñez & Gonzalez, 2009). While conflict can be healthy, it is not always managed well in the church and can result in bullying. Considering the values Christian denominations and organizations are supposed to hold, this can appear as a shock to the target and has the potential to create even greater devastation for the individual (Nuñez & Gonzalez, 2009). When these situations arise, the target feels they must endure the bullying to be considered "good Christians" (Nuñez & Gonzalez, 2009).

It was reported as many as 1,500 ministers leave the ministry each month (Muse, 2007). Conflict is consistently ranked as the greatest stressor for clergy (Hoge & Wenger, 2005), and conflict with denomination officials, church members, other pastors, church staff, and congregational leaders are some of the heaviest contributors to clergy stress (Muse, 2007). From the days of John the Baptist until now, the kingdom of heaven was subjected to violence. Such passages as Genesis 37:3-5, Jeremiah 26:20-23, Matthew 27:41-44, and Mark 15:31-32 are found throughout the New and Old Testament, demonstrating violent and aggressive behavior was a problem for the church since its formation (Wetzelberger, 2016). Bullying, which is an act that does not demonstrate love for other individuals, is contrary to the Christian virtue of love, which Jesus commanded when he said, "My command is this: Love each other as I loved you" (John 15:12) and "Love your neighbor as yourself" (Mark 12:31, New International Version).

Moral Changes and Spiritualization

While bullying has become a major concern in schools and secular workplaces, Christian organizations sometimes lag behind the general workplace in its ethics because bullying tends to be less noticeable. Christian bullies sometimes cause problems, not to mention dissension, such as organizational turmoil in faith-centered organizations (Finlan, 2015). Like bullies at children's schools and general organizations, faith-based organizational bullies can be normal, well-adjusted members of society who fall prey to destructive bullying tactics when their authority is questioned (Finlan, 2015). Some bullying behavior in faith-based organizations may result from a person's misdirected attempts at leadership, and it can sometimes be that a bully simply needs to be redirected to a healthier way of providing leadership (Finlan, 2015). Another reason Finlan (2015) noted is, as Christians reflected on their societies through time, Christian social morals have changed repeatedly. These moral changes sometimes result in not being able to determine what behaviors are deemed acceptable in Christian organizations.

Christian workplace bullying means bullying takes place and affects organizations that explicitly follow a biblical statement, the bullying may become spiritualized when illicit behaviors are rationalized by the superior objective of fulfilling the mission of the institution (Nuñez & Gonzalez, 2009). The employing organization is further able to use the employee's faith as a tool for abuse, quoting Bible texts that encourage them to be compliant or submissive (Nuñez & Gonzalez, 2009). Often, abusers in Christian organizations will quote religious or biblical concepts, such as being "called" to a specific line of work to convince the employee they are not fit for a particular job. Implied, of course, is that the employer is the sole barometer used to measure an individual's talents and abilities and that the employee should defer to this superior judgment (Nuñez & Gonzalez, 2009). Since Christian and faith-based employment is often entwined with spiritual values, employers have the added possibility of maliciously using spirituality as a tool with which to abuse targeted individuals (Finlan, 2015). Bullying can happen within the vertical hierarchies of denominations—for instance, districts, regional supervisors, district committees, and pastors who choose to bully someone of lower status to aggressively assert their power (Finlan, 2015). Finlan further asserted new ideas can be very threatening to religious authorities and bullying may be used to suppress a target's creativity or theology.

Some Christian organizations tend to be closed systems in which people work for administrators they trust but who also hold exclusive organizational power (Wetzelberger, 2016). Where there are no mechanisms for objective and independent checks, workplace abuse is more easily possible and rationalized without employees able to find help when the system mistreats them (Nuñez & Gonzalez, 2009). Religious people can practice a moralistic and judgmental kind of bullying, commonly recognized as a "holier than thou" attitude (Finlan, 2015).

Effects of Workplace Bullying in the Workplace

Yamada (2012) addressed how workplace bullying impacts organizational leadership and presented measures leaders can use to tackle this problem. He noted, although the term workplace bullying did not reach the United States until the late 1990s, the occurrence of psychologically abusive behaviors at work, and the harm created began to attract more attention from practitioners and researchers in the United States during the early to mid-1990s. The initial work came from specialists in the mental health and human resources fields, examining the impact of these behaviors on individuals and organizations (Bassman, 1992; Hornstein, 1996; Stennett-Brewer, 1997; Wyatt & Hare, 1992). In addition, a spate of "bad boss" books, often filled with anecdotes about working for horrible supervisors and intended for a more popular audience, appeared around this time (Bing, 1992; Sartwell, 1994; Tien & Frankel, 1996). The literature noted job performance and emotional well-being, health issues, and an impact on organizational costs are the major effects of workplace bullying on targets.

Job Performance and Emotional Well-Being

Namie and Namie (2009) also described how life experiences play a role in the depth of emotional injury bullying can cause a follower. They noted followers who were never abused may take longer to recognize they are being bullied. Without memories or repressed cognitive representations of abuse, bullying is a completely novel experience (Namie & Namie, 2009). Leymann's (1990) research also introduced a new aspect of workplace bullying in terms of how bullying can impact one's overall mental well-being. One of the issues for leadership professionals in every type of organization is to first understand the acts of workplace bullying and identify how bullying negatively impacts individuals and organizations (Bartlett & Bartlett, 2011). This knowledge will enable leaders to work strategically with the organization to address this concept.

Targets of workplace bullying were found to report decreased commitment, lower job satisfaction, poor morale, and lower performance/productivity (Gardner & Johnson, 2001; Namie & Namie, 2003; Yildirim, 2009). Examples of lowered performance include increase in work errors, decreased concentration, and lost time due to worrying about bullying situation (Gardner & Johnson, 2001; Namie & Namie, 2003; Paice & Smith, 2009; Yildirim, 2009). Organizations with higher incidents of workplace bullying show increased turnover, lower customer relationships, lower creativity, and lower productivity (Johnson, 2012; Namie, 2007; Namie & Namie, 2003). It is apparent workplace bullying has an overall negative impact not only on the collaborative relationships but also on the organization's productivity and reputation. Targeted workers are not the only ones negatively impacted by this mistreatment. Coworkers who witness or learn of this behavior may become intimidated and fearful, experiencing anxieties that affect the quality of their work lives as well (Namie & Namie, 2009). Targets of severe bullying are likely to bring their experiences home with them, affecting family and social relationships (Yamada, 2012). Yamada (2012) further noted people have lost their careers, livelihoods, and health due to these destructive behaviors, and too many others in positions of power and influence have chosen to ignore their pain and torment.

Health Issues

Bullying at the workplace was recognized as a risk factor in clinical depression, clinical levels of anxiety, suicide attempts, coronary heart disease, posttraumatic stress disorders, and sick leave (Matthiesen & Einarsen, 2007). Rayner and Hoel (1998) noted witnesses of bullying can also face these adverse effects as much as the target. Physiological symptoms measured by bullying consist of headaches, shortness of breath, indigestion, elevated blood pressure, and feelings of exhaustion (Hoel et al., 2010). Psychological symptoms may include restless feelings, an inability to think clearly, and irritability; behavioral symptoms might include changes in eating, sleeping, drinking, and smoking as well (Nielsen & Einarsen, 2012). At a Finnish university, in an interview study among 17 targets of bullying, Björkqvist et al. (1994) found insomnia, melancholy, various nervous symptoms, apathy, and lack of concentration were common among these bullied employees. Those effects may include the loss of sections of an active labor force through resignation, early retirement or voluntary redundancy, and the cost of medical interventions for the public health system (Oladapo & Banks, 2013).

Organizational Costs

Workplace bullying also is very bad for business (Yamada, 2012). Bassman (1992) found "employee abuse can have major bottom-line consequences" (p. 26) for employers. An employer may suffer direct costs, indirect costs, and opportunity costs as a result of abusive work environments. Direct costs include a significant increase in medical and workers' compensation claims due to work-related stress and the costs of lawsuits emerging from abusive work situations (Yamada, 2012). Because these costs are reflected in a company's financial statements, they are the easiest to measure. Research by Keashly et al. (1994) additionally showed an employer's response to complaints about bullying can influence a target's behavior at work. Targets who perceived the organizational response as being inadequate often responded with "feelings of decreased commitment and loyalty to their organization and doing the minimum work to get by" (Yamada, 2012, para. 2).

Specific Effects of Workplace Bullying in Christian Organizations

Some Christian organizations have an ethical procedure for handling grievances; however, there is not much in the way of established procedure for handling misbehavior by laity (Finlan, 2015). Employees may be made to feel they must endure the abuse to be good Christians and may be reluctant to seek legal advice. The complex feelings Christian employees have toward their organizational and personal mission and their employers can create an ideal situation for bullying to thrive. Spiritual reasons are given to justify mistreatment—and workers often suffer severe loss of self-esteem because of their failure to live up to unfair expectations created with the intentions of harm, and, at this point, the abuse can be said to be spiritualized (Nuñez & Gonzalez, 2009).

Vensel (2012) studied the impact of bullying in churches and noted the following effects on leaders, targets, and the organization:

- People who have been subjected to bullying (e.g., mobbing) in the church have experienced trauma. Trauma is cumulative—the longer the period of time it has been happening, the greater the impact on the person.

- Families are affected just as much as the person who was bullied (e.g., mobbed). This is sometimes referred to as secondary targetization. Children and especially teen who witness the bullying behavior carry the scars for a long time and often have their perceptions of God and church significantly damaged.
- Seeking help includes making formal reports to leaders or denominational representatives. Research has shown, when organizational leadership gets involved, the situation is more likely to worsen for the target than improve (i.e., 50% received no help and 25% were threatened with dismissal, a "blame the target" response).
- The person experiencing the bullying may be isolated and not receive the support they expect from those with whom they have good relationships. They experience "double betrayal" by the leaders of the church or denomination and by those they expected to support them.
- As a result of anger, exhaustion, hopelessness, or reduced commitment, targets cannot or do not produce the volume of work or the quality they produced prior to the mobbing leading to job dissatisfaction. Re-employability can be affected because of "labeling" by the denomination or influence of those giving job references to new prospective churches.
- Bullying (e.g., mobbing) experiences can have a significant negative effect on a person's worldview and their view of God, including their belief of God as a God of justice. Withdrawing from God who is the ultimate source of healing can have an impact on the recovery process.
- In the early stages of bullying (e.g., mobbing), threats to identity are linked to the loss of a sense of personal safety and self-doubt about the accuracy of perceptions about

what is happening in the church. As the bullying (e.g., mobbing) continues, targets know they are targets, and threats to identity are linked to being disbelieved, blamed, and negatively labeled. Attacks on personal and professional reputations happen at this stage. Later in the mobbing experience, threats to identity are linked to loss of a sense of being valued as a leader or professional, loss of career, and loss of beliefs about the world and God as just and fair.

Preventive Measures for Handling Workplace Bullying in Organizations

While preventive measures of workplace bullying were not assessed in this study, in this section I seek to examine the current literature and implications for future research on this phenomenon. Bartlett and Bartlett (2011) provided a recommendation on the initial assessment of bullying and the effective follow-up. Once human resource professionals and leaders are aware, policy is implemented, and work expectations are communicated, it is important for human resources professionals to be instrumental in assessing and monitoring the level of bullying in the workplace. Initial assessment can provide the organization with a benchmark to assess the growth of the organization, and constant monitoring is needed to ensure the organization is continuously providing a safe working environment. Organizational leaders must send a message that workplace bullying is unacceptable behavior (Yamada, 2012).

To understand a phenomenon as complex as workplace bullying, Yamada (2012) suggested a dynamic theoretical framework is required so organizations can ultimately prevent and/or intervene in the relevant processes. Namie and Namie (2009) recommended employers adopt a comprehensive blueprint to address bullying and this approach should include "values-driven policy" (p. 30), "credible enforcement processes" (p. 30), and "restorative interventions" (p. 31) for targets and offenders, and "general and specialized education" (p. 31). All these measures can be incorporated rather seamlessly into any productive set of existing personnel practices and policies. Namie and Namie (2009) recommended "targets" act quickly to dismantle a bullying dynamic once they recognize it, and they also urge government and judicial recognition of "bullying" as an endemic workplace issue that deserves to be taken seriously.

Yamada (2012) noted one of the most difficult decisions from both an ethical and business perspective is what to do with an abusive manager or executive as they may be seen as a "rainmaker" who is good at attracting business. In addition to clarifying management's position on the issue, like in a policy document, an understanding of leadership as a potential source of the problem needs to form part of any management training program and is also a consequence of the fact bullying only thrives when it is condoned, directly or indirectly, by management (Brodsky, 1976). Jenkins (2013) defined what an organizational policy should cover regarding workplace bullying, sexual harassment, and unlawful discrimination. His guidelines state an effective policy

- informs employees the standard of behavior outlined by the policy is enforceable.
- identifies the legislation that makes sexual harassment, discrimination, and workplace bullying unlawful.
- informs employees legal action can be taken against them for sexually harassing, discriminating against or bullying a fellow employee, or customer, and informs them they could also be exposing the organization to legal action if they carry out bullying or harassing behaviors.
- integrates with a complaints procedure that provides a range of options and a structure to address complaints of inappropriate behavior (e.g., bullying, sexual harassment and discrimination). (Jenkins, 2013, p. 42)

Ritzman (2016) also suggested intervention measures that align with Namie and Namie's (2009) "restorative interventions" approach. The interventions include ensuring employees have knowledge of workplace bullying, considering workplace bullying during recruiting and selection, developing a workplace bullying policy, establishing an avenue for employees to report complaints, imposing strict sanctions against workplace bullies, providing continual training on the topic, developing an applicable policy, and including workplace bullying in performance management initiatives (Ritzman, 2016).

Jenkins (2013) also suggested what is called a "risk management approach" to tackle workplace bullying. The first step is having a strong management commitment to the risk management approach. The organization's leadership team needs to be motivated to prevent bullying from a systemic and proactive perspective rather than a reactive perspective, or nothing will change. A proper risk management approach to preventing workplace bullying needs to be treated just as seriously by the board of directors, the chief executive officer or executive, as they would treat an approach to managing a physical hazard in the workplace (Jenkins, 2013). This fear can be manipulated by group leaders, who may attempt to foster deep feelings of loyalty to enhance an individual's sense of belonging to the group and to its leadership (Jenkins, 2013). One strategy that may be used by the bully is to allude to the other as them—that is, people who may be morally corrupt and whose thinking and behavior are unacceptable or threatening (De Souza & Mclean, 2012). Development of training specifically directed at countering bullying activities could be provided to bullies and to the personnel in the departments or locations who have been identified as having a higher incidence of bullying activities (Harvey et al., 2006).

Servant leadership can serve as a potential tool for downward and horizontal bullying as followers generally emulate how leaders behave (Yamada, 2000); therefore, not only will servant leadership help leader-to-employer bullying, it can help to prevent peer to peer bullying because servant leaders empower others and expect accountability. According to Soye (2011), the integral culture of servant leadership on an organizational level has the power to heal conflict from within, to reach outside the organization into the community in ways that promote conflict resolution. In fact, the servant leadership theory breaks from the traditional "only the strong survive" mentality and instead fosters one-on-one interventions (e.g., coaching) to maintain diversity and inclusion in the workplace (Parris & Peachey, 2013). Since servant leadership fosters more inclusive and equitable environment and practices, it is less likely for bullying to take place in an organization that fosters that leadership style because they tend to be more humane workplaces (Parris & Peachey, 2013). It is through serving that leaders lead other people to be what they can become (De Pree, 1992), which helps leaders to defeat all realms in the phenomenon of workplace bullying, because leaders set the tone for company culture.

While there is no specific research to address how leaders or followers can use their faith to help alleviate this workplace bullying issue, using faith practices is also another beneficial approach that could be recommended for Christian leaders and organizations. Cram (2003), in his text, *Bullying: A Spiritual Crisis*, challenged the Christian to reclaim the virtues of character and spiritual gifts that lead to an empathic understanding of the other. He offered four concrete practices for churches desiring to break the cycle of violence and "targetization" that leads to bullying: (a) develop a zero-tolerance bullying policy for the congregation, similar to many churches' stand on sexual misconduct; (b) take the concept of virtues into the organization; (c) promote a critical literacy toward media uses of violence; and (d) take inventory of the practices of empathy found in worship. Cram further asserted bullying takes on many forms and settings from relationships between individuals to relationships between families and nations. Despite

Cram's research being directed specifically to the church, these concepts can also be practiced in various types of organizations. Empathy, enforcing zero-tolerance policies, training, and virtue ethics would definitely be helpful in reducing this type of behavior. A final preventative measure that draws on the work of others in the area of organizational behavior management is the process-oriented A-B-C model of workplace bullying (LaVan and Martin, 2008).

The A-B-C Model

LaVan and Martin (2008) created the process-oriented model of workplace bullying. It is applicable not only in understanding the ethical aspects of workplace bullying but also in designing interventions to decrease the prevalence of workplace bullying and respond to incidents of workplace bullying in a more ethically robust manner (see Table 2). In the A-B-C model, the managers' role is essential from two perspectives: First, the manager assumes the role of a diagnostician. Second, per LaVan and Martin (2008), the manager assumes the

> role of an interventionist. When the manager is acting as a diagnostician, the manager is identifying antecedents (A), triggers, or causes behavior associated with workplace bullying. After the manager has targeted the precise antecedents (A), then the manager describes the behaviors (B) associated with workplace bullying in terms of its frequency, duration, intensity, and appropriateness, in order to formulate an intervention plan. In most instances, the manager assuming the role of the interventionist has to consider what consequences (C) or responses will be imposed upon the workplace behavior (B) being attentive to concepts like positive reinforcement, negative reinforcement and even punishment, although ill-advised. Moreover, the manager must be certain about the timing of this managerial approach to workplace bullying. (p. 150)

Table 2

Managerial Intervention Matrix

A-B-C Model	Formal	Informal
Antecedent	Investigation processes aimed at identifying triggers. Quality management processes aimed at identifying causes. EAP processes aimed at identifying vulnerability to bullying and at risk behaviors among employees who have bullied in the past. Employee selection processes aimed at identifying candidates who are more likely to be bullied at work.	Unconscious signals sent by management that bullying will or will not be tolerated. Bypassing and/or working around formal investigation, quality management, EAP, and employee selection processes aimed at identifying individuals likely to be victims of bullying at work.
Behavior	Incident report forms and tools that enable the individual completing the form to describe the behavior by level of the organization (e.g., individual, dyad, group, organizational) and to describe the behavior by specific characteristics (e.g., frequency, intensity, duration, appropriateness)	Modeling of behaviors associated with bullying or not associated with bullying.
Consequence	Disciplinary policies, procedures, and processes. Ethical and codes of conduct policies, procedures and processes. Mediation policies, procedures, and processes. EAP policies, procedures, and processes. Workplace violence policies, procedures, and processes. Grievance policies, procedures, and processes.	Conscious or unconscious reinforcement of behaviors aligned with workplace bullying or behaviors not aligned with workplace bullying. Patterns of denial in which complaints, observations, and/or tell-tale signs.

Note. From "Bullying in the U.S. Workplace: Normative and Process-Oriented Ethical Approaches," by H. LaVan and W. Martin, 2008, *Journal of Business Ethics, 83*, p. 149. Copyright 2008 by Springer.

The A-B-C model is a simple tool. Leaders can apply the A-B-C model by first organizing any data obtained from a complaint, incident report, investigation, or observation by classifying data in three categories: (a) antecedents or triggers, (b) actual behavior or bullying, and (c) consequences or response at individual, group, and organizational levels (LaVan & Martin, 2008). It is not a universal solution for dealing with all common behaviors associated with workplace bullying in both organizational contexts, but it does give some context to how manager and leaders can approach the phenomenon either by preventing or responding to it.

Summary

While the term workplace bullying has become synonymous with inappropriate workplace behaviors, the literature presented several debates as to how the phenomenon should be specifically defined and measured (Oladapo & Banks, 2013). Although a unanimous definition of workplace bullying has not been identified, researchers agree on reporting the devastating physical and mental health effects workplace bullying has on targets and witnesses, and the negative financial and cultural implications in organizational contexts. Further research on bullying from the perspective of the target is recommended to broaden the scope of workplace bullying research and to consider the voice of all participants involved in workplace bullying (Rayner & Hoel, 1998). Research on workplace bullying has encompassed self-reports from targets and bystanders and has ignored the contributions of other stakeholders (i.e., alleged perpetrator/bully); however, this study focused on the lived experiences of bullying from targets' perspectives.

Researchers of bullying consistently agree the act is systematic and repetitive (Einarsen, 1999; Leymann & Gustafsson, 1996; Rayner & Hoel, 1998) and intended to be hostile or perceived to be hostile by the target (Einarsen, 1999; Einarsen & Skogstad, 1996). Nonetheless, there was a gap in the literature related to the lived experiences of individuals, including the effect of bullying on targets and witnesses and organizational culture, especially pertaining to Christian organizations (Zapf & Gross, 2001). The literature also indicated some of the effects of bullying may overlap in both faith-centered and general organizations. For example, some of the commonalities in effects between both organizational contexts include serious health problems, poor job performance, and lack of trust in the organization (Harvey et al., 2006). However, the causes in both types of organizations have some extensive differences. For instance, workplace bullying tends to be spiritualized, and bullying is mostly described as mobbing in Christian organizations (Nunez & Gonzales, 2008). Conversely, in general organizations, bullying is more individualistic, direct, and aggressive (Einarsen & Skogstad, 1996). One key correlation is based on the scientific evidence provided by Harvey et al. (2006) linking bullying to the likelihood that those bullied have the tendency to bully, allowing these characteristics to be causes of bullying in both organizational contexts.

In terms of the preventive measures of workplace bullying, the literature has also indicated enforced human resource policies and definitive management approaches can serve as helpful leadership tools to mitigate workplace bullying in both organizational contexts (Parris & Peachey, 2013). In Chapter 3, I thoroughly describe the phenomenological method and research approach of examining workplace bullying in a Christian organization, specifically faith-based and permeated contexts. In Chapter 4, I cover the key findings of the thematic analysis, and Chapter 5 focuses on the conclusions of the study.

CHAPTER 3 – GATHERING THE STORIES

Epistemologically, phenomenological approaches are based on a paradigm of personal knowledge and subjectivity emphasizing the importance of personal perspective and interpretation (Creswell, 2013). As such, these approaches are powerful for understanding subjective experience, gaining insights into people's motivations and actions, and cutting through taken-for-granted assumptions and conventional wisdom (Glaser, Strauss, & Strutzel, 1968). Phenomenological research is a design of inquiry coming from philosophy and psychology in which the researcher describes the lived experiences of individuals related to a phenomenon, as described by participants (Creswell, 2013). Creswell (2013) noted, in phenomenological research, the researcher sets aside their experiences as much as possible to take a fresh perspective toward the phenomenon. Phenomenology is a recommended methodology when the study goals are to understand the meanings of human experiences (Creswell, 2013). Bullying is a topic that centers around a lived experience; phenomenology may help to provide more valuable insights in this social phenomenon for faith-centered organizations.

Additionally, phenomenological research aims to reveal "what it means to be human" (Creswell, 2013, p. 23) and helps researchers develop sensitivity and empathy toward their participants. A research design is the foundation and framework of a study and helps find answers to the proposed research questions (Maxwell, 2013; Miles, Huberman, & Saldaña, 2014). The decision to use this type of design was based on its flexibility, allowing for more freedom during the interview to explore essences of others' experiences (Jacobs & Furgerson, 2012; Miles et al., 2014). Researchers may use many different techniques, but central to the heart of qualitative research is the desire to expose the human part of a story (Jacobs & Furgerson, 2012). This design allowed for personal and participant expression of the lived experience of bullying in a faith-based context. A phenomenological approach is highly valuable to the understanding of all kinds of aggressive behavior (Felson & Tedeschi, 1993).

Phenomenological design in qualitative research has various strengths. One strength is the ability of the researcher to use their motivation and personal interest to fuel the study. Maxwell (2013) considered this an advantage because the researcher is motivated and has a strong interest in the topic, which supports completion of the dissertation. Another strength is how data are collected. Spoken or written accounts of personal experience gathered during the interview process is a way of yielding data (Choy, 2014; Creswell, 2013). Through subjective, direct responses, the researcher gains first-hand knowledge about what participants experience through broad and open-ended inquiry (Maxwell, 2013; Patton, 2002; Rudestam & Newton, 1992). Revisions were made along the way as new experiences emerged, giving the researcher the ability to construct themes and patterns for participants to review (Miles et al., 2014). The human factor is the greatest strength and the fundamental weakness of phenomenological qualitative inquiry and analysis—a scientific two-edged sword (Patton, 2002).

Research Approach

If qualitative research is conducted in a holistic manner, it can add more interpretive value to the researcher and the overall study (Klenke, Wallace, & Martin, 2015). Even the philosophic roots of theory are value driven and shaped by the researcher's worldview (Cederblom & Paulsen, 2012, as cited in Klenke et al., 2015). Practical implications of this philosophical basis are that qualitative methods focus on the lived experience of participants and their authentic voice, which in turn can help participants appreciate, emphasize, and promote the role of context in this study (Klenke et al., 2015). The research setting is the physical, social, and cultural site in which the researcher conducts the study. In qualitative research, the focus is mainly on meaning making; the researcher studies participants in their natural setting (Given, 2008). In this research study, participants were interviewed in a private meeting space. This approach was also beneficial to me, as the researcher, because it allowed for greater freedom of expression, and the interviewees felt freer to give an authentic answer, since the interview was not influenced by a group (Finlay, 2009).

Moustakas (1994) provided the following methods and procedures for conducting human science phenomenological research. They include:

1. Discovering a topic and question rooted in autobiographical meanings and values, as well as involving social meanings and significance;
2. Conducting a comprehensive review of the professional and research literature;
3. Constructing a set of criteria to locate appropriate coresearchers;
4. Providing coresearchers with instructions on the nature and purpose of the investigation, developing an agreement that includes obtaining informed consent, ensuring confidentiality, and delineating the responsibilities of the primary researcher and research participants, consistent with ethical principles of research;
5. Developing a set of questions or topics to guide the interview process;
6. Conducting and reporting a lengthy person-to-person interview that focuses on a bracketed topic and question (a follow-up interview may also be needed); and
7. Organizing and analyzing data to facilitate development of individual textural and structural descriptions, a composite textural description, a composite structural

description, and a synthesis of textural and structural meanings and essences.

(Moustakas, 1994, p. 103)

Moustakas's guidelines helped me understand the underpinnings of phenomenological research, specifically related to the data collection and analysis procedures from participants' perspectives. Moustakas's guidelines also served as a starting point for the thematic analysis.

Data Collection Strategies

The researcher met with participants and collected data through direct interviews using open-ended questions. Interviews provide researchers with rich and detailed qualitative data for understanding participants' experiences, how they describe those experiences, and the meaning they make of those experiences (Rubin & Rubin, 2012). Qualitative researchers can strengthen the reliability of their interview protocols as instruments by refining them through the interview protocol refinement framework, as this framework is the most suitable for refining structured or semi structured interviews (Rubin & Rubin, 2012). The four phases of the interview protocol refinement process are:

Phase 1: Ensuring interview questions align with research questions.

Phase 2: Constructing an inquiry-based conversation.

Phase 3: Receiving feedback on interview protocols.

Phase 4: Piloting the interview protocol. (Rubin & Rubin, 2012, p. 43)

Combined, these four phases offer a systematic framework for developing a well-vetted interview protocol that helps a researcher obtain robust and detailed interview data necessary to address research questions (Rubin & Rubin, 2012). Piloting the interview protocol was very beneficial to me, as the researcher, as this helped me to assess whether the questions could be applied in a faith-based workplace bullying context. Recruiting questions focused on seeking participants who experienced bullying while working in Christian faith-centered organizations within the past 10 years. To determine if they were bullied, participants' responses on the demographic questionnaire were reviewed to ensure their perceived bullying met four criteria described in the literature, which included: (a) the bullying behavior must have occurred on multiple occasions over a period, (b) an imbalance of power must have been present, (c) the bullying behavior must have been focused on one or two individuals, and (d) the bullying behavior must have been systematic (Olweus, 1993).

The researcher must do their best in the interview phase to present data and communicate what data reveal given the purpose of the study (Patton, 2002). Participants are the only ones who decide if the results reflect the phenomena being studied; therefore, it is important participants feel the findings are credible and accurate. Triangulation is a commonly used method for verifying accuracy that involves cross checking information from multiple perspectives (Klenke et al., 2015). For the purpose of this study, I selected participants from varying faith-centered organizational contexts, such as churches, Christian nonprofits, universities, and other entities that fit Sider and Unruh's (2004) standard definitions. This practice helped to safeguard the validity of the study in that different perspectives from the interviews about the lived experiences of targets of workplace bullying in faith-centered Christian organizations were highlighted. Varying perspectives give researchers the opportunity to put themselves in another person's shoes and understand the subjective experiences of each participant (Maxwell, 2013).

To obtain the most accurate data for analysis, the goal was to get a diverse group of six participants, consisting of both males and females. Creswell (2013) noted, to reduce saturation and redundancy, the size of the sample should be adequate to leave you with "nothing left to learn" (p. 218). In other words, you might conduct interviews and, after the 10th one, realize there are no new concepts emerging; that is, the concepts and/or themes begin to be redundant. Creswell (2013) further stated, in phenomenological studies, 5 to 25 participants are the right number. Therefore, six participants are within the guidelines Creswell offered. It is also argued, for qualitative research, the representation of diversity is important because the research seeks to derive information on a social phenomenon, in addition to acquiring participants from various demographics, to create more fairness in the study (Klenke et al., 2015). Also, qualitative research attempts to get mixed participant demographics, lessening the case of cultural and/or gender biases. Klenke et al. (2015) also stated research evidence should meet the needs of a diverse population; this is called internal validity, which refers to the believability and trustworthiness of the findings. Internal validity depends more on the richness of the data gathered than on the quantity of data (Maxwell, 2013).

Maximum variation sampling was used. Maximum variation sampling is a "purposeful sampling strategy in which the researcher samples cases or individuals that differ on some characteristic and then find sites or individuals with a different dimension of that characteristic" (Creswell, 2013, p. 214). The purpose of maximum variation sampling is to discover/uncover central themes, core elements, and/or shared dimensions that cut across a diverse sample while at the same time offering the opportunity to document unique or diverse variations (Creswell, 2013). To accomplish a maximum variation sample, I also recruited participants from various socioeconomic backgrounds. The nature of qualitative research often results in an everchanging research setting and changing contexts; it is important the researcher document all aspects of any changes or unexpected occurrences to further explain the findings (Klenke et al., 2015). To ensure each of the voluntary participants experienced workplace bullying, I asked preliminary demographic questions on gender, age, race/ethnicity, number of years in workplace, and the type of organization before selection. The information was obtained through the demographic and verification questionnaire (see Appendix B). This helped me to decipher whether participants were qualified, since participants under the age of 18 years old were not permitted. They were also asked to confirm the organization in which they worked to ensure it qualified as a Christian faith-centered organization. To qualify as a faith-centered organization, online research was conducted to ensure the organization was governed by faith-based or Christian principles, per Sider and Unruh (2004). If I was unable to decipher whether the organization was faith based or Christian, I placed a call to the entity and also checked the GuideStar website directory to verify if they were registered, per the faith-based guidelines.

The data collection method was a decision based on the study's underpinning that the participants to be studied and the research emphasis were the essence of human uniqueness (Patton, 2002). This means the purpose of in-depth interviewing was not to get answers to questions. At the root of in-depth interviewing is an interest in understanding the lived experiences of other people and the meaning they make of that experience (Rubin & Rubin, 2012). Interviews were confidential and allowed participants to elaborate on feelings, thoughts, and experiences pertaining to the research questions (Creswell, 2013; Miles et al., 2014; Patton, 2002). I used semi structured interviews with open-ended questions to discuss facets of workplace bullying and to determine themes. Interviewing is a strategy of collecting important information needed for analysis of the phenomenon under study (Creswell, 2013; Maxwell, 2013; Miles et al., 2014). Collectively, the semi structured interview guide provides a clear set of instructions for interviewers and can provide reliable, comparable qualitative data (Creswell, 2013).

I completed the audio recording and note taking once participants signed the consent form (see Appendix C). Interviews were conducted at a community library, which was a neutral setting for local participants able to travel to the location. The library arranged private meeting rooms on a first-come, first-served basis, so interviews were arranged for the morning periods when the rooms were likely to be available. If a participant was not in proximity or in the same city, they were offered the opportunity to conduct the interview via Zoom. If they opted to use Zoom for their interviews, participants were asked to find a quiet setting.

Interview questions were obtained from the WBI. The WBI has been in existence for over 20 years. In the United States, the WBI (2007) was the first and remains the only organization that integrates all aspects of workplace bullying: self-help advice for individuals, personal coaching, research, books, public education, union assistance, training for professionals, employer consulting, and legislative advocacy. The following 10 questions were selected from the WBI's questionnaire on workplace bullying because they are open-ended questions that allowed qualified participants to discuss their full experience with workplace bullying:

1. Describe your experience with workplace bullying in a Christian organization, specifically faith based or permeated organization?
2. What do you think was the cause(s) of the bullying?
3. Have you experienced bullying in a general organization as well? If so, what was the experience like?
4. How did you cope with the bullying experience?
5. How long ago did this experience occur?
6. Did the bully work alone or were several people bullying you?
7. What was the bully's race, gender and title in the organization?

8. Why do you believe you were targeted?
9. Did you report the bullying?
10. What was your experience after reporting the bullying? (WBI, 2007, p. 8)

Data Analysis Procedures

In each interview, I used my iPhone to minimize the amount of note taking and to devote time to listening well. I asked each participant to give their permission for the audio recording prior to the start of each session. When the Zoom platform was used for the interviews, participants were also asked to grant permission to record the interviews. Interviews lasted 30 to 60 minutes. In addition to listening, it was important to observe participants during the interview. I also transcribed interviews into written documents after I completed the interviews. There are advantages of taking written notes during an interview; however, those advantages can be diminished if participants are distracted or conversation is hindered (Meho, 2006). The interview protocol was central to the effectiveness of keeping the interviews focused. Interviewees were asked to review the transcripts after they were transcribed to maintain reliability and accuracy. This also helped to prevent any misinterpretation or bias. To ensure transcriptions were completed accurately, I used the following protocol while listening to the interview recordings, as Miles and Huberman (1994) suggested: (a) correction of any spelling or other errors; (b) anonymizing of the transcript so participants cannot be identified from anything that is said (e.g., names, places, significant events); (c) insertion of notations for pauses, laughter, and looks of discomfort; (d) insertion of punctuation (e.g., commas and periods); and (e) introduction of any other contextual information that might have affected the participant (e.g., temperature or comfort of the room).

In the analysis phase, all transcriptions from the six participant interviews were reviewed carefully by looking at written notes and reviewing the recordings. In the interview phase, transcribed summaries were labeled by themes, and participants were also identified with a code, specifically Participant 1 through 6, in lieu of using their names. The interview process provided more input to generate ideas on what participants were thinking about the subject. Creswell (2013) asserted themes are shaped into a general description in phenomenology. Thematic analysis is known as the "most commonly used analysis in qualitative research" (Creswell, 2013, p. 181). According to Guest, MacQueen, and Namey (2011), "Thematic analysis moves beyond counting explicit words or phrases and focuses on identifying and describing both implicit and explicit ideas within the data, that is, themes" (p. 8). This process helped me point out the participant's meaning as it related to the research questions. The QDA Miner Lite software was used in addition to the manual process of identifying additional themes or codes. This software program was beneficial because it helped me with the analysis of textual data for interviews through coding the data reliably (Provalis Research, 2019). Assistance provided by qualitative software can help one code and categorize large amounts of data (Yin, 2014).

QDA Miner Lite was used after each interview to analyze data through the coding and query functionalities of this software. Once the collected data were inputted, QDA Miner Lite found key words and phrases from the interviews. Once these words were ascertained, codes were organized in a tree structure that was exported from the system. After this knowledge was obtained, the interviews were categorized using themes based on the research questions. A table was also created to summarize the themes, and notes were made about how the themes were similar and different from experiences reported by each participant. A simple thematic analysis is disadvantaged when compared to other methods, as it does not allow the researcher to make claims about language use (Braun & Clarke, 2006). Even with this concern related to reliability, "a thematic analysis is still the most useful in capturing the complexities of meaning within a textual data set" (Guest et al., 2011, p. 8). Essentially, the descriptive coding method was used by labeling each theme in a table, after each interview was completed, to identify the most common threads. This was helpful in identifying major topics and unique concepts (Creswell, 2013).

Validity and Reliability

Patton (2002) stated validity and reliability are two factors about which any qualitative researcher should be concerned while designing a study, analyzing results, and judging the quality of the study. The data collection method often used in qualitative studies is interviews—face-to-face, in-depth, unstructured or structured interviews (Creswell, 2013). Research data are irreplaceable, so having a backup tool like an audio recorder for data management is essential (Maxwell, 2013; Miles et al., 2014; Patton, 2002). These tools were used in the study, thus reinforcing the validity of the study. Strengths of using a synchronous interview process are establishing rapport and homing in on the details of the interview (Creswell, 2013; Jacobs & Furgerson, 2012; Rudestam & Newton, 1992). The semistructured interviews facilitated this process. Researchers should thoroughly describe the context of the research to assist the reader in generalizing the findings and applying them appropriately (Maxwell, 2013).

Face-to face interviewing can also monitor nonverbal cues and clarify ambiguous responses (Maxwell, 2013). Getting participants involved in the process can yield positive results and large amounts of rich data (Creswell, 2013; Maxwell, 2013); however, interviewing is not a perfect method. Interviewer influence can be a limitation, which is why triangulation is needed to manage biases (Creswell, 2013). I also planned to strengthen the credibility and validity of the data through reflective listening strategies during the interview. Katz and McNulty (1994) noted:

> Reflective listening is hearing and understanding, and then letting the other know that he or she is being heard and understood. It requires responding actively to another while keeping your attention focused completely on the speaker. In reflective listening, you do not offer your perspective by carefully keep the focus on the other's need or problem. (para. 6)

This strategy enables the participant to understand the researcher is hearing accurately and create a climate of warmth (Katz & McNulty, 1994). Lastly, participants can opt out of the study, leaving one to scramble for additional participants (Jacobs & Furgerson, 2012; Patton, 2002; Rudestam & Newton, 1992). As such, more than six participants were interviewed in case one or more participants decided to withdraw from the study. Finally, there are limitations linked to credibility and reliability, or, as Rudestam and Newton (1992) advised, it is the researcher's responsibility to convince oneself and one's audience that the findings are based on critical investigation. Patton (2002) argued there are no straightforward tests that can be applied for reliability and validity. However, triangulation is typically a strategy or test for improving the validity and reliability of research or evaluation of findings (Patton, 2002). The informed consent letter and form highlighted the purpose of the study, which reinforced the value and purpose of targets participating.

Verification

Verification is the process of checking, conforming, making sure, and being certain (Morse, Barrett, Mayan, Olson, & Spiers, 2002). In other words, verification helps to identify and correct errors in the study. Methods of verification used to improve verification of this study were triangulation of data and member validation and checking. Triangulation of data refers to the use of multiple methods or data sources in qualitative research to develop a comprehensive understanding of phenomena (Patton, 2002). Patton (2002) asserted, in phenomenological studies, member validation constitutes a natural part of the dialogue between researcher and participant, as well as development of an intersubjective understanding of the phenomenon under study.

Triangulation of data was conducted using multiple sources, including interviews and analysis of existing data. Thematic content analysis was useful for the triangulation of data, as findings were compared with current theories in the literature review, such as the researched causes and effects of workplace bullying. Causes include types of leadership, organizational change and dynamics, cultural differences, personality types, and scientific evidence (Gardner & Johnson, 2001; Namie & Namie, 2003). Some of the effects of workplace bullying include change in the organizational climate, health problems for the participant and witnesses, and emotional and well-being issues (Matthiesen & Einarsen, 2007). This helped me keep data organized, thus resulting in a clearer interpretation process. The member validation process involved doing a preanalysis of the interviews, in which themes and the general story of participants' experiences were noted, after which the notes were sent to each of the six participants to ensure I interpreted participants' stories correctly. The member validation and triangulation of data processes served to verify information, which in turn enhanced the validity of the study (Miles & Huberman, 1994).

Ethical Considerations

The research was guided by the Belmont Report since human participants were involved, and it covers the protection of all research participants. All participants were treated fairly, the principle of beneficence was adhered to, and everyone involved was respected.

Vogt, Gardner, and Haeffele (2012) stressed the importance of assessing for signs of distress during research on sensitive topics and identifying strategies for minimizing discomfort. For instance, if a participant seems uncomfortable during the interview, the researcher can acknowledge they are welcome to take a break. Contrarily, Holloway and Wheeler (2002) suggested research interviews can be therapeutic even though that is not their purpose. Further consideration in phenomenological research is recognizing the lived experience of those who are recruited to participate may render them vulnerable and less able to act autonomously; therefore, it is imperative the researcher avoids exploitation of people's vulnerability (Polit & Hungler, 1999). If participants experienced any triggers from retelling their workplace bullying story, they were referred to the WBI's resources for help or to schedule an appointment with a trained counselor. The WBI also provides YouTube videos, books, free webinars, and podcasts that can assist targets with handling the experience; however, if participants were not comfortable with visiting the WBI, I advised them to schedule an appointment with a local counselor or psychologist that specializes in this issue. Additionally, if the target was still employed at the organization, I reassured them their information and participation in the study were confidential.

For the purposes of this text, I sought subjective responses from participants; therefore, the informed consent highlighted the fundamental information of the study and goals of the interview. Participants' confidentiality was protected by not using their names; instead numerical codes were used to describe them. Since participants may disclose personal information about bullying, all data were stored electronically and password protected. Participants were also reassured of confidentiality related to record storage. All records will be destroyed within 5 years of research publication, and, after usage, all data will be encrypted on a flash drive. Physical documents were stored in a locked personal office drawer.

Summary

Phenomenology was described as the primary data collection method and how semi structured interviews were used. Topics described included the research approach, participant criteria and selection, verification, validity and credibility, limitations, and ethical considerations. Methods of thematic analysis, maximum variation sampling, triangulation of data, and reflective listening helped to ensure credibility, dependability, transferability, and confirmability.

CHAPTER 4 – THE LIVED EXPERIENCES

The interview refinement protocol outlined by Rubin and Rubin (2012) was conducted to ensure the interview questions aligned with the overarching research question. This involved conducting a pilot interview to confirm the interview questions could capture participants' lived experiences. The feedback and responses gathered from the interview refinement tool phase depicted common themes, which could be established from the interview questions.

The other phase of the analysis was completed based on some of the seven phenomenological analysis steps outlined by Moustakas (1994) in Chapter 3, which were primarily organizing and analyzing data to facilitate development of individual textural and structural descriptions through a synthesis of textural and structural meanings and essences. This was accomplished by listening to interviews carefully and selecting themes that emerged from participants' experiences and researched literature. Textual data highlighted individual participants' occurrences of workplace bullying in faith-centered organizations. The final step of this stage, as outlined by Moustakas, involved assessing data collected from all of the interviews.

Findings

The main focus of this text is to understand the lived experiences of bullying targets in a faith-centered context and determined whether it is similar or dissimilar to bullying in secular organizations. I assumed the causes and effects in the organizational contexts would be vastly different. In this section, I outline major findings from the study and highlight details of each participant's story. A pseudonym is used for each participant to maintain confidentiality. Six participants, who resided in Florida, California, and South Carolina, shared their lived experiences of workplace bullying. Four participants were male, and two were female. Two participants said the bullying began with one individual, but, after reporting the incident, other managers joined in the bullying. All participants were 21 years of age or older. Also, five participants said their bullies were males, and one participant said their bully was a female. All participants mentioned their bullies were higher ranked workers or managers, while one participant said one of her bullies was higher ranked and the other was her peer.

Two participants were African American, two were Hispanic or Latino, one was Caucasian, and the other was Indian. Participants were employed in the church, faith-centered schools, and a faith-centered nonprofit. Reasons noted for targeting included one or more of the following concepts: varying spiritual beliefs, race, lack of leadership, education level, gender, and position in the organization. Table 3 presents participant demographic information. Each participant agreed to record their interviews, and the stories provide summaries based on the responses.

Table 3

Demographic Information on Research Participants

Participants	Gender	Age Range	Race/Ethnicity	Years in Workplace	Type of Organization	Reason Targeted
Participant 1 John	Male	30-39	Caucasian	1.5 years	Church	Outspoken and Differing Spiritual Beliefs
Participant 2 Maria	Female	40-49	Hispanic or Latino	4 Years	Faith-Based School	Gender, Race, and Position in the Organization
Participant 3 Josh	Male	40-49	African American	2 years	Church	Position in the Church, Stood up for Others
Participant 4 Mark	Male	30-39	Other	8 months	Faith-Based Nonprofit	Race, Culture, and Education Level
Participant 5 Juan	Male	20-29	Hispanic or Latino	8 years	Faith Based School	Lack of Leadership, Race, and Differing Spiritual Beliefs
Participant 6 Susan	Female	20-29	African American	10 years	Church	Differing Spiritual Beliefs and Abuse of Power

John's Story

A job opportunity in South Florida for a youth pastor seemed like the perfect calling for John, as a newly married and trained young minister from rural Georgia. The final interview further cemented this opportunity as the pastoral board unanimously voted for him to be their youth minister. Additionally, everyone seemed nice and welcoming during the interview process. A month after the relocation was complete, John started settling in his role but started to notice a different side of the lead pastor. He noticed, instead of instructing him during training, the lead pastor would yell if John did not understand the instructions immediately. Upon sharing his concerns with his wife, they both assumed his communication style was because he was a "New Yorker."

The yelling became worse and turned into belittling in front of others; nonetheless, John focused on his role and increased youth membership from seven to 25 members. When other members of the church started to commend John on the growth, the lead pastor would say, "Oh that's nothing," and would consistently minimize his accomplishments. The lead pastor also used his sermons to chastise John by saying subordinates should be humble and not ask questions, then stare at him when he made those comments. John spoke with the lead pastor about his common misuse of scriptures during the sermons and provided evidence to support his claims. After 6 months, the bullying impacted John emotionally, physically, and spiritually. He cried out to God, prayed, and even reported it to a board member, but nothing changed.

The final incident was nearly after a year when John decided he wanted to spend some of the professional development funds to attend a conference that would benefit some of the youth group members. The lead pastor told John he would prefer to use the $5,000 to purchase a computer. He told the lead pastor they had enough functioning computers and the money would be better spent developing the youth group. The lead pastor yelled at him saying leadership should never be questioned and started misquoting various scriptures. By this time, the youth group started to decline because John did not have the autonomy to do anything. He was deflated from dealing with his bully. John and his wife were consistently depressed about the situation and felt worse because they had no family around or a support system in the church. Ultimately, a meeting was called, and John was forced to resign. He was told the lead pastor felt he did not know what he was doing. John also worked at a general organization afterward, and when he experienced a disagreement with his manager, he felt there was a more formal human resource structure to handle the issue.

Maria's Story

Maria always dreamed of working with children. She was extremely excited when the opportunity presented itself for her to be the assistant director of her church's preschool division. In the first 6 months, she and the director grew enrollment and created a challenging curriculum that helped students exceed their goals. The church then hired a new worship leader who was exceptionally talented and charismatic. Maria excitedly introduced herself after the first service, as she knew the worship leader would also be on the church campus frequently. She was also impressed with his worship talent.

During the new worship leader's second week, he started visiting the preschool office noticeably, often under the guise he wanted to see how she was doing. One afternoon after the director left, he came by and started to stroke her shoulder. She told him that made her uncomfortable and that she was also happily married. A week later, he started coming by every evening after the director left and called her derogatory names. She was shocked this was happening and did not know to respond. After a month of dealing with the bully, she finally told her director who just cried and said she did not know what to do.

Maria decided to report the incident to the deacon and lead pastor. They told her it was best not to start trouble and that the bully was bringing a lot of people to the church. After that, the bullying intensified, and he started to call her racist names. Maria cried repeatedly, prayed, told her friends and family, got depressed, and felt hopeless. She stopped attending the church, and it affected her personal life. After almost a year, the worship leader was terminated. She found out other female minority members at the church had also experienced issues with him, and her director had also written a formal letter on her behalf. By then, she felt no justification, ended up resigning from the role, and left the church. During the interview, Maria was still visibly upset by retelling her bullying experience, and she was referred to the WBI for assistance.

Josh's Story

Josh was a police officer who was called to serve the Lord at an early age. He was ecstatic to be offered the position of the second elder in his local church. In this capacity, he worked closely with the elderly and the youth. In the first 3 months of the role, his lead pastor was reassigned, and a new pastor was assigned from their regional office. Since the new pastor's inception and upon hearing Josh was a police officer, he started to make disparaging comments about his career. Josh assumed these comments were jokes and generally ignored them. After the pastor's second month in the new role, Josh received complaints from two of the elderly members from whom the new lead pastor borrowed money—he did not pay it back in a week as he promised them. Josh decided to ask the lead pastor about it, and the lead pastor said they were not telling the truth. At the end of the sermon the following week, Josh noticed his name was taken off the leadership section of the sermon program, and, instead of greeting him with a handshake, the lead pastor elbowed him instead. Josh was in utter shock at first and assumed it was just a one-time incident. The lead pastor started to spread rumors about Josh that he was not fit to be an elder, as he was too young and did not know the word of God. Josh realized his role at the church was way more stressful than his demanding job.

He sought counsel from another elder, and she told him to pray about it. The senior elder also told him there was no point in reporting the lead pastor's behavior since he was appointed by the regional elders. Josh felt helpless and even began to question his faith because the pastor's behavior worsened. The pastor would also use his sermons to manipulate church members with virtues that were not in scripture. After the continuous bad mouthing, hostile treatment, and more complaints from the elderly regarding the lead pastor borrowing their money, Josh decided to leave the church and has since struggled with his faith.

Mark's Story

Mark was an international student who was happy to be hired in a faith-centered nonprofit organization, as he felt the experience would provide a "home away from home!" He grew up in a predominantly Christian family and was passionate about helping others. Despite his goals of being a mechanical engineer, Mark saw his role as a program manager as one he could grow to love. Upon completion of his first week of training, Mark noticed the organization was not very diverse, but he still felt welcome. Despite this, he was very friendly with everyone and felt comfortable working in a Christian environment where he could share his faith.

Mark had his first major meeting with the key managers after completing his second week. He shared his ideas and initial plans for developing the program. One of the Caucasian male managers mentioned to him that he had a very thick accent and was almost inaudible. Mark was taken aback by the comment and surprised when the other managers were chuckling loudly. After the meeting, one of the managers said to him they just liked to joke around, so he should not be embarrassed or take things personally. The next day, Mark was having lunch in the break room, and one of the managers from the same group approached him and said, "Your cousin just called me from India trying to scam me," and started laughing loudly. He left the building and took a walk outside. Mark decided to pray and ask God for wisdom.

The jokes and jeering became worse during meetings or whenever the same group of managers would see him in the workplace. Mark's work ethic gradually declined and so did his spirit. He did not know where to report the incident since the bullies were managers. His parents told him to be kind to them and laugh with them, but that did not help. Mark decided to watch Christian motivational videos to develop more strength in dealing with challenges, and he prayed earnestly and read the Bible even more than he normally would. After 8 months, Mark lost a vast amount of weight, was depressed, and felt intense anxiety every day before work. The final dealbreaker was when Mark was tasked with creating a new element of the program. During his presentation, one of the managers mimicked how he pronounced a word, and they all started laughing uncontrollably. Mark walked out of the office without offering a formal resignation.

The human resource manager called and asked him why he left in that manner, but he did not have the courage to tell her how he was treated. Since that bullying incident, Mark has never worked in another faith-centered organization.

Juan's Story

Juan sought a role in a faith-centered organization because he had experienced workplace bullying in a general organization. His church was commonly described as a "mall church" because it had over 5,000 members, a K-12 school, and even a restaurant on site. Consequently, the church had a sizeable administrative team. Juan quickly applied to an administrative position he saw advertised during their sermon notices and started the new position within 3 weeks; he hoped to escape the negative bullying experiences at his current job. Juan also felt it would afford him more opportunities to grow in his faith being around likeminded individuals.

During orientation, the director introduced himself and made it clear his first ground rule was to submit to authority. He further asserted the Bible said so, hence everyone should respect him solely without question. Juan did not give much thought to the comment at first but noticed the director misquoted several other scriptures about submitting to authority. After 2 days of training, Juan also realized the director would speak "down to him" instead of "to him." Juan asked a colleague if that was the norm, and she said the director had a military background, so he meant no harm. After the first week, the director told Juan he should not leave on time. Instead, the director told Juan it is expected, when you are working for God, one should stay late. This was concerning for Juan, as he had a newborn baby at home.

Juan stayed late every day for a week and realized the negative impact it had on his family. He did not need to stay late because his tasks were completed in his designated time at work. He decided to leave on time the following Monday. He was called in by the director

Tuesday morning and was told he was not following orders. The director yelled at him and told him employees must follow orders. Juan was confused because he worked the allotted time; nonetheless, he assumed the situation would get better since it was a faith-centered organization. The yelling, belittling, and demands for working late only got worse. If the director made a mistake, he would even tell Juan he had to do it his way. Juan noticed he was not the only person experiencing this behavior from the director but saw it was tolerated.

Juan stayed for 6 months but felt emotionally exhausted and hopeless about his faith. He prayed, cried, and read the Bible, but nothing had changed. He finally decided to file a formal report with the lead pastor and human resource administrator. They held a meeting with him and told him it was just the way his director was, and he meant no harm. He was informed to pray about it and fast. Juan resigned a week after the meeting. The most disconcerting thing for him was the bullying was similar to that of his general organizational employment, and the Bible was used to support it.

Susan's Story

Being a Sunday school teacher was something Susan said the Lord called her to do. She genuinely loved kids and felt like she could explain biblical principles in a simplistic way for them to understand. The church was family owned, but Susan always felt like a member of the family when she attended as a regular member. After a month of being a Sunday school teacher, the pastor's wife called a meeting. She said her grandson had explained an interpretation of the story of Joseph, which he learned in Sunday school, but she felt it was incorrect. Susan explained she tried to simplify the Bible stories for the kids since it was easier for them to understand. The pastor's wife started to berate her by saying Sunday school teachers should not "water down" the

Bible or misinform the kids. Susan was taken aback by the experience, but her husband told her to pray about it and not take it personally.

She prepared the following Sunday to complete her lesson but was told by the pastor's wife that they needed her to hear the sermon, so someone would fill in for her. This was shocking for Susan, but she was taught never to question her elders, especially those in the church. The pastor titled the sermon "Speaking the Truth," and Susan felt the entire message was directed at her. He mentioned "not watering down the word," speaking the truth when confronted, and ensuring kids are taught correctly about the Bible. Susan cried on the way home with her husband, as she felt embarrassed. The pastor's wife called her later that afternoon and said she hoped Susan learned the key lessons about being a good Sunday school teacher from the sermon. She also said, since Susan was now "schooled" on how to teach the Bible well, she could resume teaching next week.

Susan decided she would quit after the call. Her mom reassured her to reconsider since it is something she was passionate about. She went back the following week feeling optimistic; the criticism was behind her. Surprisingly, the pastor's wife decided to sit in on the first hour of her Sunday school session. She did not allow Susan to finish any of the lessons without interrupting. Susan decided to approach her after church ended and was told she was only trying to guide her because she was "inexperienced." The lead pastor then emailed her during the week and told her never to question his wife again, as they were the authority in the church, so she should submit to them. She responded and told the pastor she did not appreciate being critiqued so harshly. The following week, Susan was called into a meeting with the elders, the pastor, and the pastor's wife. For an hour, they berated her about how inexperienced she was at teaching. They told her she was disrespectful and noted she was not a good fit for teaching Sunday school since she could not follow instructions.

Susan was beside herself and was inconsolable during the meeting. She left the meeting feeling rejected, anxious, and depressed. For weeks she could not stop crying about the experience. The kids and other church members would ask why she was not teaching anymore, but she did not know how to respond. The pastor and his wife would lead sermons and said things she knew were directed toward her. She left the church 2 months after the meeting. Susan eventually found a new church and fearfully asked to lead Sunday school after 6 months of attending the church. She felt for sure she would fail again, but her mom inspired her with motivational videos and biblical books about hardship. Fortunately, Susan had a very positive experience in this church teaching Sunday school; however, she still felt a bit of anxiety when they called her in for meetings.

Thematic Analysis

After careful review and thematic analysis through QDA Miner Lite, eight overarching themes were discovered: (a) bullying due to race, (b) bullying due to position and gender, (c) bullying was spiritualized, (d) creating an environment of failure, (e) lack of leadership/abuse of power, (f) fear of reporting the bullying, (g) rebullying as consequence of reporting the experience, and (h) hopelessness and stress as a result of the bullying. These themes were experienced by one or more of the participants.

Theme 1: Bullying Due to Race

It is often thought race relations are not a pivotal factor in faith-centered organizations. However, Maria and Mark were bullied due to their race. Maria was called a "sand nigger" during her bullying, while Mark was ridiculed because of his accent and culture. He was even told to "go back to his home country!" Maria said she was in "utter shock" a Christian and music director for the church could utter those words much less in a faith-based organization. She went on to ask, "What's a sand nigger?" and the bully responded, "It is a Brown immigrant like you." Maria, who identifies as Hispanic, had never heard the term and told the bully she felt it was a derogatory term. However, the bully called her that name repeatedly instead of using her name when no one else was around. The WBI's (2007) research indicated Hispanics were the highest percentage of people in the workplace bullied due to their race, while African Americans were second. Despite both participants reporting the ongoing bullying due to their race, they were told by their respective managers that there was nothing they could do because they had no proof.

Rather than avoiding race, smart companies deal with it head-on—and they recognize "embracing diversity" means recognizing all races, including the majority one, to avoid showing preference or creating a backlash (Apfelbaum, 2017); nonetheless, participants who experienced bullying due to their race were never acknowledged, and the bullies were never penalized for their actions.

Theme 2: Bullying Due to Position and Gender

Those with less power in an organization are more vulnerable and prone to live through situations of harassment and mobbing because of their precarious situation (Hodson et al., 2006). Maria was told by her bully, since she was a woman, she should submit to the requests of her bully. Some argue women's advancement in working life may be perceived as challenging patriarchal power structures and therefore causes a reaction whereby increased face-to-face bullying toward women can be interpreted to retain patriarchal social control (Cortina, 2008). Susan was at a lower level position, and the bully who was her superior told her she would be relieved of her duties if she did not comply with her wishes, despite the bully's berating requests.

The participant was also threatened and told she was only a "teacher" and did not have the authority or right to question the minister's decisions. Employers may try to pressure individuals to resign by lowering the employee's salary or changing their position to create discouragement (Nuñez & Gonzalez, 2009). Employees are often powerless in situations where their paycheck is dependent on the superiors paying their salary.

Theme 3: Bullying Was Spiritualized

Juan stated his bully would say, "The Bible says you should submit to authority," and then he would misquote various scriptures to back up the concept. When Juan reported the bullying to his manager, he was told, "There is neither Jew nor Greek, there is neither slave nor free, there is no male and female, for you are all one in Christ Jesus"; therefore, it was not feasible that his teammates would bully him because of his race. Often, bullies in Christian organizations will quote religious or biblical concepts—such as being "called" to a specific line of work—to convince the employee they are not fit for a job (Nuñez & Gonzalez, 2009). When bullying is justified in a spiritual context, it creates confusion about Christian values and what is truly important in an organization that claims to work for the glory of God (Nuñez & Gonzalez, 2009). All participants noted, at some point during the bullying, a Bible verse was quoted to justify the bullying, or they were told to pray when they expressed any concern about the bullying.

John also faced backlash because he had varying spiritual beliefs with his bully. An example of this was when the bully stated the Holy Spirit is a force, and John would highlight theological viewpoints to show otherwise. The bully would then "twist" the scriptures in group meetings to attack John's viewpoint, then continuously verbally attack him by yelling and saying, "Someone here thinks they know the Bible, but they do not." Researchers have found there is a positive relationship between spirituality at work and organizational commitment, lower levels of intention to quit, intrinsic work satisfaction, job involvement, and organization-based self-esteem (Milliman, Czaplewski & Ferguson, 2003).

Theme 4: Creating an Environment of Failure

John, Josh, and Juan were repeatedly put down when they offered new suggestions or even when they performed routine tasks. Given the values Christians are supposed to hold, bullying in faith-centered contexts and organizations tends to come as a shock to employees and has the potential to create even greater devastation for the targeted individual (Nuñez & Gonzalez, 2009). For instance, Juan said if they did not do things the director's way or as perfect as he would like, he would belittle them and say, "This is not God's way, and our center will fail because you are all underperformers!"

Abusive superiors may assign tasks outside the employee's capabilities with the intent of discouraging or degrading them in their own eyes or in front of their peers. The sole purpose is to put pressure on the individual to resign. A pastor who is not "productive enough," for instance, might be sent to sell religious publications or to teach school without having the skills or background for either task (Nuñez & Gonzales, 2009). Josh was eventually asked to resign and told he was the reason why the group membership was declining, instead of increasing, despite no clear indication this was not his fault.

Theme 5: Lack of Leadership/Abuse of Power

John was engaged in a conversation with his bully who noted, "Everything in the church was for God," and John expressed the bully should not say that because the youth group will feel like God has the manifestation over everything, so they will not feel empowered. First, Christians do not believe abuse can take place in Christian organizations (Nuñez & Gonazalez,

2009). The bully, who was a minister of the church, informed John that he (the bully) was the boss and that outside of the church, he can be his friend, but that he has no say in the church. John felt leadership should be earned and not demanded. Power and its use are not a static phenomenon (Hodson et al., 2006). Oakley and Kinmond (2013) claimed the abuse of power in Christian organizations has a long-term impact on individuals, since there is a "lack of acceptance and recognition by others of the experience of it" (p. 68). John also began to distance himself from the church environment and would only attend mandatory meetings or events. Christians may distance themselves from the target because they feel uncomfortable with the stories, and they sometimes have difficulty perceiving a Christian environment as unsafe (Oakley & Kinmond, 2013).

Juan also believed there was not enough formal leadership training in the faith-centered workplace. He noted training and human resource support were more readily available in the previous general organizations he worked with. As a result, he said his bully abused his power and did not have the pertinent leadership skills to build a team. Kessler (2010) determined the following eight reasons are why it is so easy for power seekers to be influential, especially in Christian faith-centered organizations:

- Spiritual leaders have power and wherever there is power there is the potential for abuse.
- Some Christians do not believe abuse can take place in Christian organizations.
- Abuse does not fit into the moral Christian standards, resulting in the ignoring of any abusive situations.
- Many Christians have a view of humility that is conducive to abuse.

- Christians have an exaggerated need for harmony, resulting in difficulties in problem solving.
- Leadership structures in many Christian organizations are not clearly defined.
- Leaders in Christian organizations can claim the spiritual authority given to them by God, and can therefore not be questioned.
- Christian organizations attract unstable personalities looking for leaders they can look up to, resulting in unwanted abuse. (para. 3)

This "spiritual" abuse of power was evident in most of the scenarios.

Theme 6: Fear of Reporting the Bullying

All participants expressed some level of fear of reporting the bullying. Some participants opted to just keep quiet (i.e., avoidance), keep out of the way (i.e., withdrawal), or just do as they were told (i.e., ignore), but their lived experiences clearly demonstrated all of them developed distrust toward their superiors and coworkers. Only two of the six participants reported the bullying. Even when employees in faith-centered organizations realize they are being mistreated, they are often reluctant to take legal action against their employers because they have been taught Christians should not air their differences in justice halls (1 Corinthians 6:1-8, Version). When religious employers take advantage of this interpretation and use it as a harassment tool, implying or outright stating anyone who takes another Christian to trial should not be forgiven, they create an atmosphere favorable to mobbing, as it removes social support from the abused individual (Nuñez & Gonzalez, 2009). Participants also felt fearful about being terminated, mistreated, or losing their entire career if they reported the bullying. Josh also specified he was not aware of any "formal reporting structure," so there was no one to report the bullying to.

Theme 7: Rebullied as Consequence of Reporting the Experience

Workplace bullying appears to intensify, especially if the bully holds a leadership position after the target reports the bullying. Two participants shared, after reporting the bullying to the superiors, they were held under further scrutiny. John stated he was labeled a "dissenter and troublemaker," and other members of the church youth group were told not to associate with him. Juan mentioned, "I think the bullying worsened after I reported it, because, at that point, I realized reporting the bullying had no consequence for the bully"; however, the bully's tactics intensified, and he received a verbal warning, more ridicule, and no support from the workplace. Juan reported the bullying to the elders and was told "he should pray for him and that is just the way it is." The bully eventually heard and expressed to Juan that God is going to curse him, because he is the authority there, and he disrespected authority.

Theme 8: Hopelessness and Stress as a Result of the Bullying

All participants reported adverse emotional effects of the lived experiences of workplace bullying. They all cried, felt hopeless, and also experienced extreme stress because of the bullying. Only one participant sought counseling, and most used prayers as a coping mechanism or scripture as a means of emotional support. A perceived sense of closeness to God is particularly valuable to spiritual people in stressful and difficult situations (Hill & Pargament, 2003). Participants felt alienated from the rest of their coworkers and also were intentionally excluded from day-to-day work activities. Susan mentioned other people in the organization who were also bullied felt hopeless and that there was nothing they could do to resolve the situation because the bully made them feel inadequate. Participants reported they had "serious headaches," stomach pains, and a high level of anxiety when they thought about work or were present in the organization. Maria even mentioned suffering hair loss from stress and feeling hopeless about life in general. All participants reported sleepless nights and the debilitating lived experience of bullying also seeping into their personal lives. Susan said she was even angrier at her son, and he would say to her, "Mommy what's wrong?" and "You're like a monster!" She then realized it was time to resign from the position.

Chapter Summary

In sum, all six participants described themselves as hardworking, committed Christians, and ethical workers. A few of them even referred to themselves as "strong willed" individuals. Nonetheless, their lived experiences of being bullied in a faith-centered organization were described as the most horrific professional experiences and even the worst experience of their lives. They all expressed the same argument that they were disheartened and shocked to realize bullies even exist in faith-centered organizations. Some participants claimed, despite the bullying occurring years ago, they would not like to work in a faith-centered context again. Two participants were still reeling from the negative impacts of bullying, as they were extremely tearful and sad about the experience.

The findings aligned with Olweus' (1993) definitions of workplace bullying, specifically that bullying is repeated, bullying represented an imbalance of power, and bullying behavior was often systematic. Data from this study offers value to researchers, organizational conflict practitioners, faith-based leaders and managers, policymakers, Christian organizations, and general organizations regarding recognition, support, and mitigation of workplace bullying.

CHAPTER 5 – CONCLUSION

In this chapter, I summarize the lived experiences of workplace bullying in faith-centered organizations. I also focus on answers to the research questions based on the study's findings and discuss a comparative analysis of bullying in faith-centered and general organizations, as well as implications of the study for both organizational contexts. In this chapter, I also offer viewpoints on the study's contributory relevance to the literature of workplace bullying in faith-centered organizations and discuss a future research approach from which the study may benefit. I conclude with a summary of the underpinnings of the study.

Results in Light of the Study's Research Questions

While the research has shown workplace bullying is predominant in general organizations, only one short study (Nuñez & Gonzalez, 2009) looked at "mobbing" in Christian organizations. This study's focus was to explore the lived experiences of people experiencing workplace bullying in faith-centered organizations, which is a different context from bullying in the general workplace setting. Considering no phenomenological studies on the lived experiences of workplace bullying were found on bullying in a faith-centered organization, the need to explore this study's research questions was vast. Underlying research questions focused on factors that contributed to the bullying, causes and effects of workplace bullying in general and faith-centered organizations, and whether workplace bullying is similar or dissimilar in each of the organizational contexts.

Findings obtained from participants were meaningful in responding to the research questions. All participants reported their lived experiences of workplace bullying in faith-centered organizations were very negative. Causes and effects of bullying were similar in general organizations, but there were some stark dissimilarities, which will be discussed in the next section. Lived experiences of workplace bullying were investigated in two ways. Initially, I researched workplace bullying for both organizational contexts in the literature review and found there are significant causes of workplace bullying, such as cultural differences, organizational culture, and imbalance of power. Effects such as psychological distress, health problems, poor job performance, and lack of trust in the organization were found in the literature review. Upon completion of the data analysis, the study's answers were comparable with findings in the literature. The literature review reinforced the importance of how a positive organizational culture and leadership can help to mitigate workplace bullying in both organizational settings. The review also highlighted how the opposite can cause bullying in organizations. Participants expressed that faith-centered leaders encouraged bullying, as bullying went unaddressed by leaders. S. J. Hogan and Coote (2013) found organizational culture influenced behaviors; participants in this study further asserted culture starts from the top and goes downward, and leaders must be proactive to have positive cultures. The thematic analysis confirmed and supported findings of Georgakopoulos, Wilkin, and Kent (2011) that organizational cultures worsened the problem of bullying as leaders were indifferent to bullying and their actions or lack of actions reinforced it.

The themes were also meaningful in answering Questions 3 and 4, as they confirmed and aligned with the body of knowledge indicated by S. J. Hogan and Coote (2013), who found organizational culture was an invisible yet powerful means used to elicit desired organizational outcomes. The text also found toxic leaders played a critical role in promoting toxic cultures, which could unknowingly promote bullying (Cleary, Walter, Andrew, & Jackson, 2013). Some participants noted, even when bullying was reported to the faith-centered leaders, their reports were ignored or excuses were made on the bullies' behalf. Ignored workplace bullying practices then became an accepted part of the organization's culture (Georgakopoulos et al., 2011). Kellerman (2004) further argued leadership goes wrong more often than not in what appears to be a reverse pyramid from benign to malignant, which is cataloged as the seven deadly sins of leadership: (a) incompetence, (b) rigidity, (c) intemperance, (d) callousness, (e) corruption, (f) insularity, and (g) evil. Despite the belief this type of toxic leadership is not the norm in faith-centered organizations, this trajectory of toxic leadership was evidenced in all participants' stories. Participants were either chastised, fired, or asked to resign by leaders at some point in relation to the bullying.

The literature also indicated conflict, moral changes, and spiritualization are the more specific factors of bullying in a faith-centered context (Nuñez & Gonzalez, 2009); however, the findings specified the lived experiences of workplace bullying in faith-centered organizations were like bullying in general organizations, as causes noted in the literature were expressed by participants, except for spiritualization and moral changes. Despite those similarities, the study signified participants in faith-centered contexts handled bullying differently by using spiritual coping mechanisms, and those in a general workplace setting resort to reporting bullying, but preventive measures were necessary for leaders and managers in both organizational contexts.

Comparison of Bullying in Faith-Based and General Organizations

Per the literature review and in response to Questions 4 and 5, the effects of bullying were similar in general and faith-centered organizations, with some dissimilarities with the bullying in both organizations; however, participants who experienced bullying in general organizations felt they had more formal structures for reporting bullying. Some causes were also similar, such as bullying due to race, abuse of power, and gender. The stark difference is bullying was not spiritualized in general organizations, and scriptures were not used to justify treating targets poorly. Two participants also reported they were mistreated in a general organizational setting and did not expect bullying to happen in a faith-centered organization. Existing literature on general workplace bullying also substantiated that targets handled bullying differently in general organizations. All participants used their faith and religion to help them cope with bullying in the faith-centered organizations.

Pargament et al. (1992) found religious coping is multidimensional, identifying four themes of religious beliefs, behaviors, support, and motivations helpful to those who involve religion in the coping process:

- Belief in a just and loving God. Appraisals of events as reflective of God's will and orthodox beliefs in a just and merciful personal God was predictive of positive outcomes to negative events. Feelings of anger and distance from God and other church members were related to poorer outcomes.
- Experience of God as a supportive partner. The individual's relationship with God is experienced as personal and intimate as opposed to abstract, emotion focused, and problem focused. Coping involves personal effort while recognizing the limits of personal agency. God is viewed as able to offer help in the coping process and plays a special supportive role when the individual is faced with the limits of personal control through the knowledge that the deity will be there to make events endurable.
- Involvement in religious rituals was also associated with positive outcomes. Rituals included the attendance of religious services, prayer, Bible reading, and attempts to live a less sinful, more loving life. Individuals may attempt to influence outcomes through the ritual acknowledgment that the problem is in the hands of God thus reducing the need for personal control.

- Search for spiritual and personal support through religion. Positive outcomes were associated with an intrinsically motivated approach to religion, where individuals look to God for closeness and guidance in dealing with problems.

Participants mentioned a few of these religious coping mechanisms were helpful in that their relationships with God helped them during the bullying to not go into further despair, or, for some, it brought them closer to God. Regardless, participants also noted further preventive measures, such as leadership and human resource, would have helped to mitigate some of the psychological stress they experienced. Additionally, the study indicated, when targets of bullying reported the bullying, they felt there was a need for action in terms of stricter antibullying laws. Despite this, Kalman (2012) stated:

> Antibullyism teaches that we need to fight for antibullying laws, as though laws can force us to like and respect each other. Jesus is a fierce opponent of the legal approach to conflict. He makes this clear throughout the Sermon, repeatedly contrasting what the law tells us with his own instructions. Antibullyism insists that we need anti-bullying laws so that the fear of being sued will make our bullies want to treat us like friends. We conveniently forget that these same laws can be used by others against us, for to them we are the bullies. (para. 4)

Since there is an absence of federal legislation prohibiting workplace bullying, managers and leaders must develop preventive measures to assist targets and potential bullies with measures for handling it. In the next section, preventive measures will be examined to suggest potential solutions to workplace bullying.

Per the requirements of a phenomenological methodology, a small sample size was used for this study. To determined more context around the lived experiences of workplace bullying in faith-centered organizations, a larger mixed method study would be recommended as both a continuation of this dissertation effort and as a platform to capture the other categories of Christian organizations (e.g., faith-permeated, faith-affiliated, faith-background, and faith-secular partnership; Sider & Unruh, 2004). It would also be intriguing to conduct research on managers and leaders who handled bullying in faith-centered and general organizations. This would help to provide a more practical approach to handling workplace bullying in both organizational contexts. Despite the coping skills targets may have found useful in faith-centered contexts, there is more that can be done to make employees feel protected.

Implications

In their study, "Mobbing in Christian Organizations: When Abuse Is Spiritualized," Nuñez and Gonzalez's (2009) examined 10 participants across different countries in Christian organizations on their perceptions of workplace bullying and whether it was spiritualized. The authors concluded the important spiritual mission of a Christian institution does not negate the need to preserve the dignity and value of the individuals who work there (Nuñez & Gonzalez, 2009). This was consistent with findings that highlighted workplace bullying as a persistent reality in faith-centered organizations, even if there were policies that prohibited the behavior. Even more disturbing is the seemingly widespread acceptance in these organizations of the idea one also must tolerate abuse to be a good Christian (Nuñez & Gonzalez, 2009). Arguably, effects demonstrated by participants' lived experiences were similar to responses offered by mobbing participants in Nuñez and Gonzalez's findings. Workplace bullying in faith-centered organizations has adverse effects, specifically concerning the lack of Christian organizational support

Additionally, whether the bullying was reported, the targets felt it was spiritualized. Concerning bullying being spiritualized, the targets who identified as Christians struggled even more because they viewed their bullies as individuals created with love by God. As with discussions about improving any workplace—for instance, with introducing diversity such as gender and race representation—the context of workplace bullying should be approached with a more elaborate policy process that is supported from different directions (i.e., from the public, the organization, educational institutions, and worker buy-in), so workplace bullying is minimized and eventually eliminated (Oade, 2009). In terms of the reported workplace bullying, having a strong integrative policy (i.e., teaching about antibullying at all levels of citizens' education) may be useful for reassuring employees their presence and contribution to organizations are always valued (Oade, 2009), thus resulting in a happier, more productive workforce in any organizational context.

Another evident implication was, in some faith-centered organizations, there is an accepted level of abusive behavior by superiors; therefore, there are inadequate policies on workplace bullying. The other issue is some faith-centered organizations may have policies, but the leadership and organizational culture does not enforce or support these policies. The third possibility lies in the fact leadership is aware and polices exist, but the bully brings extensive value to the organization and therefore is "untouchable." If these behaviors are common occurrences, then it is feasible findings from this study imply employees will not have a positive experience after reporting their bullying experience. An additional challenge is some of the faith-centered organizations retaliated against the target by labeling them, forcing them to resign, or maybe even terminating them. This proved very difficult for participants, as they all reported feeling some loss of dignity, whether they reported the bullying or not.

Another implication drawn from reviewing the findings revealed, because participants were not given any kind of support by the respective faith-centered organization, they had nothing positive to say about the organization. This implied there was a connection between a breakdown of the relationship between managers and subordinates but also within the organization. This can result in the organization getting a bad reputation, especially since faith-centered organizations are held to higher standards in terms of how they are expected to treat their employees. In the findings, it was evident participants confided in friends, family, and even members of the same organization that created a negative perception of that particular workplace. In essence, faith-centered organizations that tolerate workplace bullying may encounter negative reviews, and this can affect their public persona, especially for places of worship. The evident indications of fear, humiliation, therapy, and alienation due to workplace bullying highlight the intensity of challenges reported in the lived experiences of employees who have experienced bullying in faith-centered organizations. This study also recognized those who lived the experience of workplace bullying generally extended their psychological and physical issues to those closest to them, thus resulting workplace bullying being a social reality rather than an isolated phenomenon. The overall implication of these findings is the need for more effective workplace bullying policies in faith-centered organizations.

Conclusion

Workplace bullying is a complex organizational phenomenon with ethical implications, both within and outside any given organization in which workplace bullying occurs (LaVan & Martin, 2008). Initially, definitions of workplace bullying were explored, and organizational frameworks in general and in Christian organizations were also determined. After developing the questions to consider and selecting faith-centered organizations as the context for the text, the next step was to investigate the literature on why bullying occurred in general and in faith-centered settings. The effects of bullying were also discovered in both contexts, and the nature and the various aspects of bullying were clarified. This text found workplace bullying in faith-centered organizations affected not only the targets but also the witnesses and the organization as whole.

The findings point to the fact bullying is generally spiritualized in faith-centered organizations, and coping skills, in addition to the level of reporting, are somewhat more informal in this setting; however, the causes and effects of workplace bullying were similar to those in a general organization, which all resulted in painful experiences for participants. Themes were also supported by concepts found about the causes and effects of workplace bullying in a faith-centered organization. It also helped to confirm development of the negative effects workplace bullying has on participants in faith-centered organizations. The findings and literature also suggested, while organizations may be aware of the negative influence workplace bullying has on the overall organizational culture and climate, it has not declined; therefore, more measures need to be implemented to promote a workplace where every employee is treated with dignity and respect.

REFERENCES

Adams, A. (1992). *Bullying at work: How to confront and overcome it.* London, England: Virago.

Adams, J. S. (1965). Inequity in social exchange. In L. Berkowitz (Ed.), *Advances in experimental social psychology* (Vol. 2, pp. 267–299). New York NY: Academic Press.

Alsgaard, E. (2013, August). Bullying happens in church. Don't ignore it. *Intrepid Magazine.* Retrieved from www.interpretermagazine.org/topics/bullying-happens-in-church.-dont-ignore-it

Althaus, P. (1966). *The theology of Martin Luther.* Philadelphia, PA: Fortress Press.

Andersson, L., & Pearson, C. (1999). Tit for tat? The spiraling effect of incivility in the workplace. *Academy of Management Review, 24,* 452–471. doi:10.5465/amr.1999.2202131

Apfelbaum, M. I. N. E. (2017, March 24). The costs of racial "color blindness." *Harvard Business Review.* Retrieved from https://hbr.org/2013/07/the-costs-of-racial-color-blindness

Aquino, K. (2000). Structural and individual determinants of workplace targetization: The effects of hierarchical status and conflict management style. *Journal of Management, 26,* 171–193. doi:10.1177/014920630002600201

Aquino, K., & Byron, K. (2002). Dominating interpersonal behavior and perceived targetization in groups: Evidence for a curvilinear relationship. *Journal of Management, 28,* 69–87. doi:10.1177/014920630202800105

Association of Religion Data Archives. (2010). *Religious congregations and membership in the United States, 2000*. Retrieved from Association of Religion Data Archives website: http://www.thearda.com/mapsReports/reports/US_2000.asp

Baillien, E., Neyens, I., De Witte, H., & De Cuyper, N. (2009). Qualitative study on the development of workplace bullying: Towards a three-way model. *Journal of Community & Applied Social Psychology, 19*, 1–16. doi:10.1002/casp.977

Barna Research Group. (2011). *A profile of Protestant pastors in anticipation of "Pastor Appreciation Month."* Retrieved from https://www.barna.com/research/a-profile-of-protestant-pastors-in-anticipation-of-pastor-appreciation-month/

Baron, R., & Nueman, J. (1998). Workplace violence and workplace aggression: Evidence concerning specific forms, potential causes, and preferred targets. *Journal of Management, 24*, 391–419. doi:10.1177/014920639802400305

Bartlett, J. E. (2016). Workplace bullying: A silent epidemic. *HRMagazine, 59*(10), 22–23.

Bartlett, J. E., & Bartlett, M. E. (2011). Workplace bullying: An integrative literature review. *Advances in Developing Human Resources, 13*, 69–84. doi:10.1177/1523422311410651

Bassman, E. (1992). *Abuse in the workplace: Management remedies and bottom line impact.* Westport, CT: Quorum.

Bernardin, H. (2012). *Human resource management* (6th ed.). New York, NY: McGraw Hill/Irwin.

Bies, R. J., & Moag, J. F. (1986). Interactional justice: Communication criteria of fairness. In R. J. Lewicki, B. H. Sheppard, & M. H. Bazerman (Eds.), *Research on negotiations in organizations* (Vol. 1, pp. 43–55). Greenwich, CT: JAI Press.

Bing, S. (1992). *Crazy bosses.* New York, NY: Pocket Books.

Björkqvist, K., Österman, K., & Hjelt-Bäck, M. (1994). Aggression among university employees. *Aggressive Behavior, 20*, 173–184. doi:10.1002/1098-2337(1994)20:3<173: aid-ab2480200304>3.0.co;2-d

Booth, A., Johnson, D. R., Granger, D. A., Crouter, A. C., & McHale, S. (2003). Testosterone and child and adolescent adjustment: The moderating role of parent-child relationships. *Developmental Psychology, 39*, 85–98. doi:10.1037/0012-1649.39.1.85

Bordia, P., Hobman, E., Jones, E., Gallois, C., & Callan, V. (2004). Uncertainty during organizational change: Types, consequences, and management strategies. *Journal of Business & Psychology, 18*, 507–532. doi:10.1023/B:JOBU.0000028449.99127.f7

Bosworth, K., Espelage, D. L., & Simon, T. R. (1999). Factors associated with bullying behavior in middle school students. *Journal of Early Adolescence, 19*, 341–362. doi:10.1177/0272431699019003003

Bowling, N. A., & Beehr, T. A. (2006). Workplace harassment from the victim's perspective: A theoretical model and meta-analysis. *Journal of Applied Psychology, 91*, 998–1012. doi:10.1037/0021-9010.91.5.998

Branch, S., Ramsay, S., & Barker, M. (2013). Workplace bullying, mobbing and general harassment: A review. *International Journal of Management Reviews, 15*, 280–299. doi:10.1111/j.1468-2370.2012.00339

Braun, V., & Clarke, V. (2006). Using thematic analysis in psychology. *Qualitative Research in Psychology, 3*, 77–101. doi:10.1191/1478088706qp063oa

Brodsky, C. M. (1976). *The harassed worker*. Toronto, Ontario, Canada: Lexington Books.

Carden, L. L., & Boyd, R. O. (2010). Workplace bullying: An ethical context applying duty and outcome-based approaches to human resource functions. *Southern Journal of Business and Ethics*, *2*, 144–150. doi:10.1007/10551-012-1468-2

Caspi, A., McClay, J., Moffitt, T. E., Mill, J., Martin, J., Craig, I. W., . . . Pulton, R. (2002). Role of genotype in the cycle of violence in maltreated children. *American Association for the Advancement of Science*, *297*(5582), 851–854. doi:10.1126/science.1072290

Chaves, M. (1994). Secularization as declining religious authority. *Social Forces*, *72*, 749–744. doi:10.2307/2579779

Choy, L. T. (2014). The strengths and weaknesses of research methodology: Comparison and complimentary between qualitative and quantitative approaches. *Journal of Humanities and Social Science*, *19*(4), 99–104. Retrieved from http://www.iosrjournals.org/iosr-jhss/papers/Vol19-issue4/Version-3/N0194399104.pdf

Cleary, M., Walter, G., Andrew, S., & Jackson, D. (2013). Negative workplace behaviours at the University of Hard Knocks. *Contemporary Nurse, 44,* 253–256. doi:10.5172/conu.2013.44.2.253

Collinson, D. L. (1988). "Engineering humour": Masculinity, joking and conflict in shop-floor relations. *Organization Studies, 9,* 181–199. doi:10.1177/017084068800900203

Cortina, L. M. (2008). Unseen justice: Incivility as modern discrimination in organizations. *Academy of Management Review, 33,* 55–75. doi:10.1177/0149206311418835

Cowie, H., Naylor, P., Rivers, I., Smith, P. K., & Pereira, B. (2002). Measuring workplace bullying. *Aggression and Violent Behavior, 7,* 33–51.

Coyne, I., Craig, J., & Smith-Lee Chong, P. (2004). Workplace bullying in a group context. *British Journal of Guidance & Counselling, 32*, 301–317. doi:10.1080/03069880410001723530

Coyne, I., Seigne, E., & Randall, P. (2000). Predicting workplace target status from personality. *European Journal of Work and Organizational Psychology, 9*, 335–349. doi:10.1080/135943200417957

Cram, R. H. (2003). *Bullying: A spiritual crisis*. St. Louis, MO: Chalice Press.

Crawford, J. (1999) The relationship between commitment and organizational culture, subculture, leadership style and job satisfaction in organizational change and development. *Leadership & Organization Development Journal, 20*, 365–377. doi:0.1108/01437739910302524

Creswell, J. W. (2013). *Qualitative inquiry and research design: Choosing among five approaches* (3rd ed.). Los Angeles, CA: Sage.

Davenport, N., Schwartz, R. D., & Elliot, G.P. (1999). *Mobbing: Emotional abuse in the American workplace*. Ames, IA: Civil Society.

De Pree, M. (1992). *Leadership jazz*. New York, NY: Dell.

De Souza, M., & McLean, K. (2012). Bullying and violence: Changing an act of disconnectedness into an act of kindness. *Pastoral Care in Education, 30*, 165–180. doi:10.1080/02643944.2012.679955

Einarsen, S. (1999). The nature and causes of bullying at work. *International Journal of Manpower, 20*, 16–27. doi:10.1108/01437729910268588

Einarsen, S., Hoel, H., Zapf, D., & Cooper, C. (2003). The concept of bullying at work. In S. Einarsen, H. Hoel, D. Zapf, & C. Cooper (Eds.), *Bullying and emotional abuse in the workplace: International perspectives in research and practice* (pp. 3–31). London, England: Taylor & Francis.

Einarsen, S., & Skogstad, A. (1996). Bullying at work: Epidemiological findings in public and private organizations. *European Journal of Work and Organizational Psychology, 5*, 185–201. doi:10.1080/13594329608414854

Escartín, J., Zapf, D., Arrieta C., & Rodriguez-Carballeira, A. (2011). Workers' perception of workplace bullying: A cross-cultural study. *European Journal of Work and Organizational Psychology, 20*, 178–205. doi:10.1080/13594320903395652

Felson, R. B., & Steadman, H. J. (1983). Situational factors in disputes leading to criminal violence. *Criminology: An Interdisciplinary Journal, 21*(1), 59–74. doi:10.1111/j.1745-9125.1983.tb00251.x

Felson, R. B., & Tedeschi, J. T. (Eds.). (1993). *Aggression and violence: Social interactionist perspectives.* Washington, DC: American Psychological Association.

Ferris, P. A. (2009). The role of the consulting psychologist in the prevention, detection, and correction of bullying and mobbing in the workplace. *Consulting Psychology Journal, 61*, 169–189. doi:10.1037/a0016783

Field, T., & Field, M. (2005). Bullying: What is it? Types of bullying, bullying tactics, how targets are selected, the difference between bullying and harassment: An answer to the question "Why me?" *Bully Online.* Retrieved from http://www.bullyonline.org/workbully/bully.htm

Finlan, S. (2015). *Bullying in the churches.* Eugene, OR: Wipf and Stock.

Finlay, L. (2009). Debating phenomenological research methods. *Phenomenology & Practice, 3*, 6–25. doi:10.1007/978-94-6091-834-6_2

Fox, S., & Stallworth, L. E. (2005). Racial bullying: Exploring links between bullying and racism in the U.S. workplace. *Journal of Vocational Behavior, 66*, 438–456. doi:10.1016/j.jvb.2004.01.002

Gardner, S., & Johnson, P. R. (2001). The leaner, meaner workplace: Strategies for handling bullies at work. *Employment Relations Today, 28*(2), 23–36. doi:10.1002/ert.1012

Georgakopoulos, A., Wilkin, L., & Kent, B. (2011). Workplace bullying: A complex problem in contemporary organizations. *International Journal of Business and Social Science, 2*(3). Retrieved from http://ijbssnet.com/

Given, L. M. (Ed.). (2008). *The Sage encyclopedia of qualitative research methods*. Thousand Oaks, CA: Sage.

Glanzer, P. L., & Ream, T. C. (2009). *Christianity and moral identity in higher education: Becoming fully human*. New York, NY: Palgrave MacMillan.

Glaser, B., Strauss, A., & Strutzel, E. (1968). The discovery of grounded theory: Strategies for qualitative research. *Nursing Research, 17*, 350–364. doi:10.1097/00006199-196807000-00014

Glasø, L., Matthiesen, S. B., Nielsen, M. B., & Einarsen, S. (2007). Do targets of workplace bullying portray a general target personality profile? *Scandinavian Journal of Psychology, 48*, 313–319. doi:10.1111/j.1467-9450.2007.00554.x/full

Guest, G., MacQueen, K., & Namey, E. (2011). *Applied thematic analysis*. Thousand Oaks, CA: Sage.

Hamel, G., & Prahalad, C. K. (1994). Competing for the future. *Harvard Business Review, 72*(4), 122–128. Retrieved from https://hbr.org/1994/07/competing-for-the-future

Harvey, M. G., Heames, J. T., Richey, R. G., & Leonard, N. (2006). Bullying: From the playground to the boardroom. *Journal of Leadership & Organizational Studies, 12*(4), 1–11. doi:10.1177/107179190601200401

Hauge, L., Skogstad, A., & Einarsen, S., (2010). The relative impact of workplace bullying as a social stressor at work. *Scandinavian Journal of Psychology, 51*, 426–433. doi:10.1111/j.1467-9450.2010.00813

Haynie, D. L., Nansel, T., Eitel, P., Crump, A. D., Saylor, K., Yu, K., & Simons-Morton, B. (2001). Bullies, targets, and bully/targets: Distinct groups of at-risk youth. *Journal of Early Adolescence, 21*, 29–49. doi:10.1177/0272431601021001002

Hepworth, W., & Towler, A. (2004). The effects of individual differences and charismatic leadership on workplace aggression. *Journal of Occupational Health Psychology, 9*, 176–185. doi:10.1037/1076-8998.9.2.176

Hershcovis, M. S., Reich, T. C., Parker, S. K., & Bozeman, J. (2012). The relationship between workplace aggression and target deviant behavior: The moderating roles of power and task interdependence. *Work & Stress, 26*, 1–20. doi:10.1080/02678373.2012.660770

Hill, P. C., & Pargament, K. I. (2003). Advances in the conceptualization and measurement of religion and spirituality: Implications for physical and mental health research. *American Psychologist, 58*, 64-74. doi:10.1037/0003-066X.58.1.64

Hitt, M. A., Keats, B. W., & DeMarie, S. M. (1998). Navigating in the new competitive landscape: Building strategic flexibility and competitive advantage in the 21st century. *Academy of Management Executive, 12*, 22–42. doi:10.5465/ame.1988.1333922

Hodson, R., Roscigno, V. J., & Lopez, S. H. (2006). Chaos and the abuse of power: Workplace bullying in organizational and interactional context. *Work and Occupations, 33*, 382–416. doi:10.1177/0730888406292885

Hoel, H., Glasø, L., Hetland, J., Cooper, C. L., & Einarsen, S. (2010). Leadership styles as predictors of self-reported and observed workplace bullying. *British Journal of Management, 21*, 453–468. doi:10.1111/j.1467-8551.2009.00664.x

Hoel, H., & Salin, D. (2003). Organizational antecedents of workplace bullying. In S. Einarsen, H. Hoel, D. Zapf, & C. Cooper (Eds), *Bullying and emotional abuse in the workplace: International perspectives in research and practice* (pp. 71–83). London, England: Taylor & Francis.

Hogan, R., Raskin, R., & Fazzini, D. (1990). The dark side of charisma. In K. E. Clark & M. B. Clark (Eds.), *Measures of leadership* (pp. 343–354). West Orange, NJ: Leadership Library of America.

Hogan, S. J., & Coote, L. V. (2013). Organizational culture, innovation, and performance: A test of Schein's model. *Journal of Business Research, 67*, 1609–1621. doi:10.1016/j.jbusres.2013.09.007

Hoge, D., & Wenger, J. (2005). *Pastors in transition*. Grand Rapids, MI: Eerdmans.

Holloway, I., & Wheeler, S. (2002) *Qualitative research in nursing* (2nd ed.). Oxford, England: Blackwell Science.

Hornstein, H. (1996). *Brutal bosses and their prey: How to identify and overcome abuse in the workplace*. New York, NY: Riverhead.

Hutchinson, M., Wilkes, L., Jackson, D., & Vickers, M. H. (2010). Integrating individual, work group and organizational factors: Testing a multidimensional model of bullying in the nursing workplace. *Journal of Nursing Management, 18*, 173–181. doi:10.1111/j.1365-2834.2009.01035

Jacobs, S., & Furgerson, S. P. (2012). Writing interview protocols and conducting interviews: Tips for students new to the field of qualitative research. *The Qualitative Report, 17*(6), 1–10. Retrieved from http://www.nova.edu/ssss/QR/QR17/jacob.pdf

Janesick, V. J. (2011). *"Stretching" exercises for the qualitative researcher* (3rd ed.). Thousand Oaks, CA: Sage.

Jenkins, M. (2013). *Preventing and managing workplace bullying and harassment: A risk management approach.* Sydney, Australia: Academic Press.

Johnson, C. E. (2012). *Meeting the ethical challenges of leadership: Casting light or shadow* (4th ed.). Thousand Oaks, CA: Sage.

Kalman, I. (2012). Jesus taught the solution to bullying. *Psychology Today.* Retrieved from https://www.psychologytoday.com/us/blog/resilience-bullying/201212/jesus-taught-the-solution-bullying

Karasek, R. (1979). Job demands, job decision latitude, and mental strain: Implications for job redesign. *Administrative Science Quarterly, 24*, 285–308. doi:10.2307/2392498

Katz, N., & McNulty, K. (1994). *Reflective listening.* Syracuse University. Retrieved from http://www.maxwell.syr.edu/uploadedFiles/parcc/cmc/Reflective Listening NK.pdf

Keashly, L., Trott, V., & MacLean, L. M. (1994). Abusive behavior in the workplace: A preliminary investigation. *Violence and Targets, 9*, 341–357. doi:10.1037/10893-009

Kellerman, B. (2004). *Bad leadership: What it is, how it happens, why it matters*. Cambridge, MA: Harvard Business School Press.

Kessler, V. (2010). Leadership and power. *Koers Bulletin for Christian Scholarship, 75*, 527–550. doi:10.4102/koers.v75i3.95

Kinney, J. (1995*). Faces by National Safe Workplace Institute*. Chicago, IL: Worldcat.

Koonin, M., & Green, T. M. (2005) The emotionally abusive workplace. *Journal of Emotional Abuse, 4*(3), 71–79. doi:10.1300/J135v04n03_05

Klenke, K., Wallace, J. R., & Martin, S. M. (2015). *Qualitative research in the study of leadership*. Wagon Lane, England: Emerald Group.

LaVan, H., & Martin, W. (2008). Bullying in the U.S. workplace: Normative and process-oriented ethical approaches. *Journal of Business Ethics, 83*, 147–165. doi:10.1007/s10551-007-9608-9

Lewis, D., & Gunn, R. (2007). Workplace bullying in the public sector: Understanding the racial dimension. *Public Administration, 85,* 641–665. doi:10.1111/j.1467-9299.2007.00665.x

Leymann, H. (1990). Mobbing and psychological terror at workplaces. *Violence and Targets*, *5*, 119–126. doi:10.1037/a0016590

Leymann, H., & Gustafsson, A. (1996). Mobbing at work and the development of post-traumatic stress disorders. *European Journal of Work and Organizational Psychology*, *5*, 251–275. doi:10.1080/13594329608414858

Leventhal, G. S. (1980). What should be done with equity theory? New approaches to the study of fairness in social relationships. In K. Gergen, M. Greenberg, & R. Willis (Eds.), *Social exchange: Advances in theory and research* (pp. 27–55). New York, NY: Plenum Press.

Liefooghe, A. P., & Mac Davey, K. (2010). Accounts of workplace bullying: The role of the organization. *European Journal of Work and Organizational Psychology, 10*, 375–392. doi:10.1080/13594320143000762

Lutgen-Sandvik, P. (2003). The communicative cycle of employee emotional abuse: Generation and regeneration of workplace mistreatment. *Management Communication Quarterly, 16*, 471–501. doi:10.1177/0893318903251627

Masters, M. F., & Albright, R. R. (2002). *The complete guide to conflict resolution in the workplace.* New York, NY: American Management Association.

Matthiesen, S. B., & Einarsen, S. (2007). Perpetrators and targets of bullying at work: Role stress and individual differences. *Violence and Targets, 22*, 735–753. doi:10.1891/088667007782793174

Maxwell, J. A. (2013). *Qualitative research design: An interactive approach* (3rd ed.). Thousand Oaks, CA: Sage.

Meho, L. (2006). E-mail interviewing in qualitative research: A methodological discussion. *Journal of the American Society for Information Science and Technology, 57*, 124–129. doi:10.1002/asi.20416

Miles, M. B., & Huberman, A. M. (1994). *Qualitative data analysis: An expanded sourcebook.* Thousand Oaks, CA: Sage.

Miles, M. B., Huberman, A. M., & Saldaña, J. (2014). *Qualitative data analysis: A methods sourcebook* (3rd ed.). Thousand Oaks, CA: Sage.

Miller, W. R., & Seligman, M. E. (1975). Depression and learned helplessness in man. *Journal of Abnormal Psychology, 84*, 228–238. doi.org/10.1037/h0076720

Milliman, J., Czaplewski, A. J., & Ferguson, J. (2003). Workplace spirituality and employee work attitudes. *Journal of Organizational Change Management, 16*, 426–447. doi:10.1108/09534810310484172

Mitchell, M. S., & Ambrose, M. L. (2007). Abusive supervision and workplace deviance and the moderating effects of negative reciprocity beliefs. *Journal of Applied Psychology, 92*, 1159–1168. doi:10.1037/0021-9010.92.4.1159

Morrill, C. (1992). Organizational conflict management as disputing process: The problem of social escalation. *Human Communication Research, 18*, 400–428. doi:/10.1111/j.1468-2958.1992.tb00558.x

Morse, J. M., Barrett, M., Mayan, M., Olson, K., & Spiers, J. (2002). Verification strategies for establishing reliability and validity in qualitative research. *International Journal of Qualitative Methods, 1*(2), 13–22. Retrieved from http://ejournals.library.ualberta.ca/index.php/IJQM/article/view/4603/3756

Moustakas, C. (1994). *Phenomenological research methods*. Thousand Oaks, CA Sage.

Mullin-Rindler, N. (2003). *Findings from the Massachusetts Bullying Prevention Initiative*. Retrieved from Health Resources and Services Administration website: http://www.stopbullyingnow.hrsa.gov/

Murray, J., & Segal, D. (1994). Emotional processing in cognitive therapy and vocal expression of feeling. *Journal of Social and Clinical Psychology, 13*, 189–206. doi:10.1521/jscp.1994.13.2.189

Muse, S. (2007). Clergy in crisis: When human power isn't enough. *Journal of Pastoral Care & Counseling, 61*, 183–195. doi:10.1177/154230500706100303

Namie, G. (2007). The challenge of workplace bullying. *Employment Relations Today, 34*(2), 43–51. doi:10.1002/ert.20151

Namie, G., & Namie, R. (2003). *The bully at work: What you can do to stop the hurt and reclaim your dignity on the job* (Rev. ed.). Naperville, IL: Sourcebooks.

Namie, R., & Namie, G. (2009). *The bully at work: What you can do to stop the hurt and reclaim your dignity on the job* (2nd ed.). Naperville, IL: Sourcebook.

Nielsen, M. B. & Einarsen, S. (2012). Outcomes of exposure to workplace bullying: A meta-analytic review. *Work & Stress, 26*, 309–332. doi:10.1080/02678373.2012.734709

Northouse, P. C. (2004). *Leadership: Theory and practice*. Newbury Park, CA: Sage.

Nuñez, M. A., & Gonzalez, S. (2009). Mobbing in Christian organizations: When abuse is spiritualized. *Journal of Applied Christian Leadership, 3*(2), 33–47.

Oade, A. (2009). *Managing workplace bullying: How to identify, respond to and manage bullying behavior in the workplace*. New York, NY: Palgrave Macmillan.

Oakley, L., & Kinmond, K. (2013). *Breaking the silence on spiritual abuse* (Kindle ed.). London, England: Palgrave Macmillan.

Oladapo, V., & Banks, L. T. (2013). Management bullies: The effect on employees. *Journal of Business Studies Quarterly, 4*(4), 107-120. Retrieved from http://www.jbsq.org/

Olweus, D. (1993). *Bullying at school: What we know and what we can do*. Oxford, England: Blackwell.

Paice, E., & Smith, D. (2009). Bullying of trainee doctors is a patient safety issue. *The Clinical Teacher, 6,* 13–17. doi:10.1111/j.1743-498X.2008.00251.x

Pargament, K., Olsen, H., Reilly, B., Falgout, K., Ensing, D., & Van Haitsma, K. (1992). God help me (II): The relationship of religious orientations to religious coping with negative life events. *Journal for the Scientific Study of Religion, 31*, 504-513. doi:10.2307/1386859

Parris, D., & Peachey, J. (2013). A systematic literature review of servant leadership theory in organizational contexts. *Journal of Business Ethics, 113*, 377–393. Retrieved from http://www.jstor.org/stable/23433856

Patton, M. Q. (2002). *Qualitative research & evaluation methods* (3rd ed.). Thousand Oaks, CA: Sage.

Polit D. F., & Hungler, B. P. (1999). *Nursing research: Principles and methods* (6th ed.). Philadelphia, PA: Lippincott Williams and Wilkins.

Provalis Research. (2019). *Introducing QDA Miner Lite*. Retrieved from https://provalisresearch.com/products/qualitative-data-analysis-software/freeware/

Raine, A., Buchsbaum, M. S., Stanley, J., Lottenberg, S., Abel, L., & Stoddard, J. (1994). Selective reductions in prefrontal glucose metabolism in murderers. *Biological Psychiatry, 36*, 365–373. doi:10.1016/0006-3223(94)91211-4

Ramsay, S., Troth, A., & Branch, S. (2011). Workplace bullying through the lens of social psychology: A group level analysis. *Journal of Occupational and Organizational Psychology, 84*, 799–816. doi:10.1348/2044-8325.002000

Rayner, C., & Hoel, H. (1998). A summary review of literature relating to workplace bullying. *Journal of Community and Applied Social Psychology, 7*, 181–191. doi:10.1002/(SICI)1099-1298

Ritzman, M. (2016). A phenomenon we can't ignore: Performance improvement interventions to address workplace bullying. *Performance Improvement, 55*, 14–22. doi:10.1002/pfi.21545

Roscigno, V. J., Lopez, S. H., & Hodson, R. (2009). Supervisory bullying, status inequalities and organizational context. *Social Forces, 87*, 1561–1589. doi:/10.1353/sof.0.0178

Rubin, H. J., & Rubin, I. S. (2012). *Qualitative interviewing: The art of hearing data* (3rd ed.). Thousand Oaks, CA: Sage.

Rudestam, K. E., & Newton, R. R. (1992). *Surviving your dissertation: A comprehensive guide to content and process.* Thousand Oaks, CA: Sage

Salin, D. (2003). Ways of explaining workplace bullying: A review of enabling, motivating and precipitating structures and processes in the work environment. *Human Relations, 56*, 1213–1232. doi:10.1177/00187267035610003

Samnani, A. K., & Singh, P. (2016). Workplace bullying: Considering the interaction between individual and work environment. *Journal of Business Ethics, 139*, 537–549. doi:10.1007/s10551-015-2653

Saltmarsh, M. (2007, February 5). The workplace: It's called mobbing – Business – International Hearld Tribune. *The New York Times.* Retrieved from https://www.nytimes.com/2007/02/05/business/worldbusiness/05iht-workcol06.4474372.html

Sartwell, M. (1994). *Bosses from hell: True tales from the trenches.* New York, NY: Penguin

Saunders, P., Huynh, A., & Goodman-Delahunty, J. (2007). Defining workplace bullying behaviour professional lay definitions of workplace bullying. *International Journal of Law & Psychiatry, 30*, 340–354. doi:10.1016/j.ijlp.2007.06.007

Schwartz, D., Dodge, K. A., & Coie, J. D. (2003). The emergence of chronic peer targetization in boys' play groups. *Child Development, 64*, 1755–1772. doi:10.1111/j.1467-8624.1993.tb04211.x

Schutz, A. (2014). The phenomenology of the social world. *Journal of the British Society for Phenomenology, 2*(3), 81–84. doi:10.1080/00071773.1971.11006206

Sheehan, M. (1999). Workplace bullying: Responding with some emotional intelligence. *International Journal of Manpower, 20*, 57–69. doi:10.1108/01437729910268641

Sheehan, M., Barker, M., & Rayner, C. (1999). Applying strategies for dealing with workplace bullying. *Journal of Manpower, 20*, 50–57. doi:10.1108/01437729910268632

Sider, R. J., & Unruh, H. R. (2004). Typology of religious characteristics of social service and educational organizations and programs. *Nonprofit and Voluntary Sector Quarterly, 33*, 109–134. doi:10.1177/0899764003257494

Silverman, D. (2006). *Interpreting qualitative data: Methods for analyzing talk, text and interaction* (3rd ed.). London, England: Sage.

Simon, C., & Simon, D. (2006). Bully for you: Full steam ahead: How Pennsylvania employment law permits bullying in the workplace. *Widener Law Journal, 16*, 141–164.

Soye, P. A. (2011). Corporate integrity and company-community conflict management in the Niger delta region of Nigeria. *Journal of Leadership, Accountability & Ethics, 8*(3), 77–88.

Sperry, L. (2009). Workplace bullying and mobbing: The influence of individual, work group, and organizational dynamics on abusive workplace behavior. *Consulting Psychology Journal: Practice and Research, 61*, 190–201. doi:10.1037/a0016938

Stennett-Brewer, L. (1997). *Trauma in the workplace: The book about chronic work trauma.* Decatur, IL: Nepenthe.

Tengilimoğlu, D., Akdemir Mansur, F., & Dziegielewski, S. F. (2010). The effect of the mobbing on organizational commitment in the hospital setting: A field study. *Journal of Social Service Research, 36,* 128–141. doi:10.1080/01488370903578082

Tepper, B. J., Moss, S. E., & Duffy, M. K. (2011). Predictors of abusive supervision: Supervisor perceptions of deep-level dissimilarity, relationship conflict, and subordinate performance. *Academy of Management Journal, 54,* 279–294. doi:10.5465/amj.2011.60263085

Tien, E., & Frankel, V. (1996). *The I hate my job handbook: How to deal with hell at work.* New York, NY: Ballantine Books.

Torry, M. (2014). *Managing religion: The management of Christian religious and faith-based organizations.* New York, NY: Palgrave MacMillan.

Tracy, S. J., Lutgen-Sandvik, P., & Alberts, J. K. (2006). Nightmares, demons, and slaves: Exploring the painful metaphors of workplace bullying. *Management Communication Quarterly, 20,* 148–185. doi:10.1177/0893318906291980

Vartia, M. A. (2001). Consequences of workplace bullying with respect to the well-being of its targets and the observers of bullying. *Scandinavian Journal of Work, Environment & Health, 27,* 63–69. doi:10.5271/sjweh.588

Vensel, S. R. (2012). *Mobbing, burnout, and religious coping styles among Protestant clergy: A structural equation and its implications for counselors* (Doctoral dissertation). Retrieved from http://purl.flvc.org/FAU/3356893

Vogt, W. P., Gardner, D. C., & Haeffele, L. M. (2012). *When to use what research design*. New York, NY: Guilford Press.

Vorster, N. (2015). Just war and virtue: Revisiting Augustine and Thomas Aquinas. *South African Journal, 34*, 55–68. doi:10.1080/02580136.2015.1010135

Weisel, M. (2016). Bullying in the workplace: Not every wrong has a legal remedy. *Labor Law Journal, 67*, 520-528.

Wetzelberger, T. (2016). *Supporting anti-bullying in church environments: A program evaluation study* (Doctoral dissertation). Retrieved from ProQuest Dissertations and Theses database. (Order No. 10253648)

Woodrow, C., & Guest, D. (2017) Leadership and approaches to the management of workplace bullying. *European Journal of Work and Organizational Psychology, 26*, 221–233. doi:10.1080/1359432X.2016.1243529

Workplace Bullying Institute (WBI). (2007). *The 2007 U.S. Workplace Bullying Survey*. Retrieved from http://workplacebullying.org/multi/pdf/WBIsurvey2007.pdf

Wyatt, J., & Hare, C. (1992). *Work abuse: How to recognize and survive it*. Rochester, VT: Schenkman.

Yamada, D. C. (2012). Workplace bullying and ethical leadership. *Journal of Values-Based Leadership, 1*(2), 49–62. doi:10.1008/10551-015-2654

Yamada, D. C. (2000). The phenomenon of "workplace bullying" and the need for status-blind hostile work environment protection. *Georgetown Law Journal, 88*(3), 475–536. doi:10.1891/088667007782793174

Yildirim, D. (2009). Bullying among nurses and its effects. *International Nursing Review, 56*, 504–511. doi:10.1111/j.1466-7657.2009. 00745.x

Yin, R. (2014). *Case study research design and methods* (5th ed.). Thousand Oaks, CA: Sage.

Yukl, G. (2000). *Leadership in organizations* (4th ed). Englewood Cliffs, NJ: Prentice Hall.

Zapf, D., Escartin, J., Einarsen, S., Hoel, H., & Vartian, M. (2010). Empirical findings on prevalence and risk groups of bullying in the workplace. In S. Einarsen, H. Hoel, D. Zapf, & C. Cooper (Eds.), *Bullying and harassment in the workplace: Developments in theory, research and practice* (2nd ed., pp. 75–106). London, England: Taylor & Francis.

Zapf, D., & Gross, C. (2001). Conflict escalation and coping with workplace bullying: A replication and extension. *European Journal of Work and Organizational Psychology*, *10*, 497-522. doi:10.1080/13594320143000834

www.ingramcontent.com/pod-product-compliance
Lightning Source LLC
Chambersburg PA
CBHW050012230526
45465CB00003BB/1381